MW01242957

# Transforming Your Story

# Transforming Your Story

*A Path to Healing after Abortion*

CHPC
Washington, DC

Unless otherwise indicated, Scripture quotations are from the Holy Bible, New Living Translation (NLT). Copyright 1996. Used by permission of Tyndale House Publishers Inc. All rights reserved.

Scripture quotations marked AMP are from The Amplified Bible. Copyright 2015 by the Lockman Foundation. Used by permission. All rights reserved.

Scripture quotations marked HCSB are from the Holman Christian Standard Bible. Copyright 1999, 2000, 2002, 2003, 2009 by Holman Bible Publishers. Used by permission. All rights reserved.

Scripture quotations marked MSG are from The Message. Copyright 1993, 1994, 1995, 1996, 2000, 2001, 2002 by Eugene H. Peterson. Used by permission of NavPress Publishing Group. All rights reserved.

Scripture quotations marked NCV are from the New Century Version. Copyright 2005 by Thomas Nelson Inc. Used by permission. All rights reserved.

Scripture quotations marked NIV are from the Holy Bible, New International Version. Copyright 1973, 1978, 1984, 2011 by Biblica Inc. Used by permission. All rights reserved worldwide.

Scripture quotations marked NIV 84 are from the Holy Bible, New International Version. Copyright 1984, 1995 by International Bible Society. Used by permission of Zondervan. All rights reserved.

Scripture quotations marked NRSV are from the New Revised Standard Version Bible. Copyright 1989 by the Division of Christian Education of the National Council of the Churches of Christ in the United States of America. Used by permission. All rights reserved.

© 2018 by Capitol Hill Pregnancy Center and Wendy Giancola

All rights reserved. This book or any portion thereof may not be reproduced or used in any manner whatsoever without the express written permission of the publisher, except for the use of brief quotations in a book review.

Printed in the United States of America

Capitol Hill Pregnancy Center
713 Maryland Ave NE
Washington, DC 20002
http://www.transformingyourstory.org


Book packager: Garrett Brown, Merrifield Press
Typesetting: Robin Black, Inspirio Design
Copyediting: Kristen Stieffel and Corrie Schwab
Cover and interior design: David Carlson, Studio Gearbox
Text set in Garamond Premier Pro and Gotham

# CONTENTS

*I will return her vineyards to her*
*and transform the Valley of Trouble*
*into a gateway of hope.*

—Hosea 2:15

# How to Use This Book

*Transforming Your Story* began as the personal recovery component to biblically based healing groups at the Capitol Hill Pregnancy Center in Washington, DC. It developed from both my personal story and the journeys of other women I met along the way, and it is intended to be used in the context of a supportive, confidential small group focused on recovering from the emotional and spiritual pain of abortion. The chapters build on each other to help women process the layers of grief and pain that build up following an abortion, so it is best to go through the topics in order and not skip ahead.

Based on our experience over several years, we believe optimal healing includes three important aspects: community, spiritual tools, and prayer.

## Community

Your story is transformed as you participate in a fellowship of honest reflection. Sharing one's story with others has incredible healing power, as it breaks isolation and reinforces a sense of belonging and understanding. You can share it with others in a healing-group setting or one on one, depending on your comfort level and circumstances and the availability of a group near you.

I strongly recommend that you join a healing group to facilitate your journey through recovery. A confidential group can break your isolation and lessen your fear and sadness. You also learn and grow when you share honestly with others while supporting and encouraging one another. Resources to help you locate a group are found on page 179. A sample group commitment form is found on page 143 to clarify group dynamics.

If you are unable to find a group and are reading this book on your own, I urge you to invite at least one trustworthy and compassionate friend—preferably more—to support and pray for you on this path to recovery and perhaps join you for activities along the way. The encouragement and patient listening of another person is invaluable as you process a range of emotions.

For women considering facilitating a group, a facilitator's companion is available as a free PDF download from the book's website. It provides guidance and enhanced activities for groups as they work through each chapter toward the goal of transforming their stories. My colleagues and I highly recommend using the companion in conjunction with this guidebook, since it provides discussion points and questions as well as enhanced practical activities for each step on the path.

This book has been designed to reinforce that sense of community and connectedness to other women's experiences. At the end of each chapter, past participants share their personal testimonies and reflections.

> A person standing alone can be attacked and defeated, but two can stand back-to-back and conquer. Three are even better, for a triple-braided cord is not easily broken.
>
> —Ecclesiastes 4:12

## SPIRITUAL TOOLS

The chapters in this book are constructed around stories from the Bible. You, the reader, are invited to delve into the Bible story and to view your own story through its lens. This is accomplished through personal questions that encourage contemplation. The "Let's Talk" sections serve as prompts for personal reflection and application and as points for group discussion.

It may be helpful to keep a journal or other writing instrument nearby to allow thoughts, ideas, and emotions to flow freely as Scriptures are read and your personal story is examined. This involves your thinking, feeling, and behavior, so a variety of spiritual tools can be helpful to engage all aspects. This book provides spaces throughout for your thoughts, prayers, and responses, as well as some additional journaling space at the back.

In addition to the stories, this book provides practical tools and ideas throughout to help you heal. These tools can typically be applied to other aspects of your personal story in addition to abortion recovery. Each chapter also includes a "Make It Personal" activity that involves the heart, mind, body, and spirit. These activities reinforce a concept from the chapter and are adapted for individuals to complete alone within this book. However, the activities are most effective when completed in a group, as in the enhanced version provided in the facilitator's companion. Chapters conclude with an encouragement to "Journey Further" by opening up a Bible and reading a psalm related to the chapter's topic. Many psalms are actually prayers, and prayer is a vital component to healing.

> Draw near to God, and He will draw near to you.
>
> —James 4:8 (HCSB)

## PRAYER

In addition to communicating with others in some way, it is imperative to communicate with God to transform your story. Prayer is simply communicating with God, talking with Him, whether out loud or in the quietness of your mind and heart. Prayer does not require special, complicated words or formulas. It is being willing to share your heart and mind with God honestly, whatever that may involve. It is also being open to God's response, however He may communicate it—through a person, a reading, journaling, or something else.

Prayer is calling out to God, seeking to make a connection. God wants us to connect with Him before we do anything, so pray (ask) for guidance before you begin this book and as you work through each chapter. Pray or talk to God even if you doubt whether you are heard. Share your doubts, fears, and hopes, or simply say or think "Help!" or "Thank you!" Each chapter includes a thought about prayer or a suggestion for prayer. Prayer is the primary means of growth and healing, so try it repeatedly!

As you hike this path of recovery, our prayers and hearts are traveling with you. God is also with you, and through this journey, your story of difficulty will be transformed into a gateway of hope!

> Call to me and I will answer you and tell you great and unsearchable things you do not know.
>
> —Jeremiah 33:3 (NIV)

# LAURIE

*A Story of Pulling Weeds*

One day I asked my four-year-old niece to help me weed my community garden plot, since she likes getting her hands dirty. I explained that we were pulling the weeds so we could make rows and plant seeds that will grow into the vegetables she likes.

As I was weeding, I noticed out of the corner of my eye that my niece was re-planting flower-looking weeds like dandelion and clover. I stopped her and explained again that we were pulling the weeds so we could plant something else.

I continued to weed, and again saw her re-planting them in a small corner of the plot. I asked her to not re-plant the weeds, and she began to cry because they were "pretty flowers," not weeds.

As she cried, I took her into my lap. "You know I love you, and because of that I want the best for you, right?"

Through sniffles, she said, "Yes."

"I know you like the flowers, but do you also want to plant lots of the yummy healthy vegetables you like?"

With big eyes, she responded, "Yes!"

"Those flowers are actually yucky weeds that can harm our vegetables and prevent them from growing. It is sad and difficult to pull the flower weeds now, but once we do, we can plant all those wonderful vegetables and they will be able to grow so we can enjoy them and share them with our family and friends. Are you willing to help me pull the flower weeds so we can grow those great vegetables to enjoy later?"

Slowly she smiled and said, "Yes!"

What a great metaphor for the healing path we take to transform our story. At times we look at the story of our life and notice that a few "flowers" have sprung up around our abortion episode. They seem somewhat pretty, so we leave them just where they are or place them strategically throughout our story. We don't want to really examine them to determine whether they are helpful.

Over time, we realize there is little else growing or thriving in our story. The "flowers" of loss, sadness, frustration, and guilt seem to be growing well, though. In fact, the roots are going deeper into fear, anger, bitterness, depression, and shame. The "flowers" are growing into destructive thoughts and behaviors. Soon they crowd out and maybe destroy healthy "vegetables" like relationships, opportunity, hope, and peace. What seemed like pretty flowers are weeds that are choking out the healthy aspects of a good life story.

We can choose to leave the flowers in place, or believe that God loves us and wants the best for us, which means examining and pulling up a few flowery weeds along this path so the good vegetables can grow and be enjoyed.

Perhaps, like me, you view your abortion episode as one of the lowest, most difficult valleys of your life story thus far. You have allowed the "flowers" to trouble and burden the path of your life. Are you willing to cooperate with God to pull the weeds? It was not a quick, easy task for me, but the tasty "vegetables" I have gained thus far were worth it. Better still, I now know there is even more to come! He can and will restore your life's garden.

# A TROUBLED STORY

*Do not be far from me,*
*for trouble is near*
*and there is no one to help.*
—PSALM 22:11 (NIV)

Who doesn't love a good story? We love to read stories, listen to stories, watch stories, and tell stories. We like different kinds of stories about different kinds of people, places, and situations. We love stories because our lives are stories. Multiple episodes are woven together in a unique and interesting life story for each of us.

We like to remember and share some of our personal episodes. As we share them with family and friends, we enjoy laughter over a fun, well-lived story. But some episodes we don't want to remember. Some of us have a more troubled tale that we don't share with others. It is well hidden in the dark corners of the heart and mind. This episode is kept safely under lock and key, to be shared with no one, often not even with ourselves.

Around the world, millions of women of childbearing age have life stories that include at least one abortion episode. The reasons for having an abortion are as various as the unique episodes that compose our life stories, and they are influenced by and rooted in those episodes. Numerous pressures, fears, situations, and difficulties, whether imposed by self or by others, pile up until the choice is made and the abortion chapter is added.

Although abortion is legal and ostensibly socially acceptable, many of us who have had an abortion don't want to talk about it, so we keep our story secret. When we first had the abortion, perhaps we thought, *at least the "crisis" of unplanned pregnancy is over!* Then other thoughts and feelings may have started to creep into our hearts and minds, sometimes slowly, sometimes like a flood.

Some women may unexpectedly experience a range of confusing emotions and reactions in response to the procedure. Some women may feel "sadness, grief, and feelings of loss" following an abortion.[1] Abortion does involve loss: loss of expectations, of a child, of opportunity, of relationships. These losses deserve to be grieved. Yet some of us who have had an abortion may feel we have no right to grieve our loss for a variety of reasons. Reasons may include internal messages such as self-blame (*it was my own fault*) and external messages such as social acceptance (*it was the right thing to do; you should not feel bad*).

Instead of grieving, we may push grief down, denying it is even there, becoming emotionally numb or "dead." We may think we are moving on as we think we should. Some of us become so angry or guilty that we have problems with relationships. We may feel so empty that we try to fill the void with anything we can: food, drugs, sex, shopping, work, and more.

Too often women have no idea these emotions and behaviors are related to their abortion, so they stay silent and tolerate the discomfort or try to cope with the outward behaviors without considering or grieving the abortion. Some of us may experience such intense emotion and pain that we fear we may be crazy. Either way, we keep this episode of our life story in the dark.

Perhaps you picked up this book because something triggered you to remember the abortion episode after years of keeping it buried. Or perhaps you've been struggling with the pain ever since it happened, or you have tried to cope with the emotions and behaviors, but still feel stuck. Perhaps some people or institutions in your life have told you abortion was the "right thing" or it was "no big deal," so you are afraid to talk with them, unsure of how they would react to your feelings. Maybe you blame only yourself, and fear telling anyone who may reject you, so you feel totally alone. You may be wondering whether you are the only one who has ever felt this way or thought these things following an abortion. You don't know where to turn, so you did the "safe" thing, and picked up a book.

Whatever brought you to this point, know that I too have experienced the same confusion and fear. After I kept my abortion story "successfully" hidden for many years, some things triggered my memory and a flood of emotion came. At first, I wasn't sure how and in what ways my abortion influenced my life story, and I was surprised to learn how far-reaching the impact was. I began to connect feelings and behaviors to that shadowy darkness in my life story.

Maybe you aren't aware of exactly how your life has been affected by your abortion decision, either. I encourage you to consider the following questions to help you shine some light into the darkness of your abortion story.

## Where Are You?

Put a check mark by those things you have experienced since your abortion and those that may have been intensified or influenced by the abortion experience.[2]

❑ Do you avoid the subject of abortion, or do you become upset or uncomfortable if the subject comes up, whether among friends, in the news, or elsewhere?

❏ Do you find yourself trying to forget your abortion(s)?

❏ Do you feel sad or depressed since the abortion, or do you cry a lot?

❏ Are you angry and resentful with people who were involved in your abortion decision?

❏ Do you feel guilty, afraid, ashamed, or unworthy since the abortion?

❏ Have you withdrawn socially, or do you feel a sense of loneliness or isolation?

❏ Are you uncomfortable around babies or pregnant women? Or do certain sounds or places bother you?

❏ Do you have trouble building or maintaining relationships? Do you avoid relationships, or do you become overly dependent on them? Do you get involved in hurtful relationships?

❏ Do you feel emotionally numb or dead? Are you unable to experience feelings?

❏ Has your self-concept or self-esteem changed since the abortion?

❏ Have you experienced an increase in harmful behaviors such as
- casual sex and promiscuity?
- eating disorders or food issues?
- abuse of drugs, alcohol, or other substances?
- self-harming behaviors, such as cutting?

❏ Have you had nightmares or flashbacks related to your abortion experience?

❏ Are there certain times of the year when you feel sick, sad, or distracted, such as on the anniversary of the abortion?

❏ Are you uncomfortable with physical or emotional intimacy?

❏ If you have children, do you overprotect them? Do you struggle to bond with or enjoy your children?

❏ If you don't have children, are you obsessed about having them or concerned about your ability to have them?

❏ Have you encouraged others to get an abortion after you had yours?

❏ Do you strive for success (in career, relationships, or education) or overcommit to "prove" abortion was the right choice?

❏ Do you feel a vague sense of emptiness or sense of loss?

❏ Do you feel differently about yourself since the abortion? Have you lost interest in things you once enjoyed?

PAS, or Post-abortion Syndrome, is a term developed by researchers Anne C. Speckhard and Vincent M. Rue, who suggest that a pattern of some of these behaviors and emotional reactions may be linked to an abortion experience.[3] PAS involves an inability to fully process the pain and come to peace with an abortion experience, resulting in emotional and behavioral changes affecting the present. One study found that women who have had an abortion "face higher rates of anxiety, depression, and heavier alcohol and marijuana use."[4] The abortion experience may be sensed as a trauma that can be likened to a jellyfish, in that the tentacles of the event still sting and can reach into your present and pull you back into the pain of the past.

Every person is unique and experiences the effects of abortion differently. Perhaps you identify with very few of these questions and feel little sadness or concern. Or perhaps you identify with many of them, as I did. I felt a sense of relief and validation—and of hope for healing—from naming my feelings and reactions as PAS. Maybe the terms *trauma* or *syndrome* offend you or make you uncomfortable. That is not the intent. Please do not let any discomfort you have with such terms deter you from this important point: The aftermath of abortion impacts many women around the world, so if you believe it is part of your story, you are not alone. You are not crazy.

PAS can be like a physical sickness in that it can affect you in serious ways. If you had a physical sickness or syndrome and if there were no barriers to going to a doctor, would you go to a doctor for treatment and healing? If you didn't go, what do you think would happen? Or do you think the effects could get worse? How much of your life could end up being affected?

Ultimately, the questions boil down to two: What do you do with this new awareness of the impacts of the abortion experience? What would it take for you to decide to seek recovery and healing?

## TRANSFORMING OUR STORIES

For me, it took fifteen years of experiencing PAS symptoms before I realized I needed help. Just as with a physical sickness, unless you see the problem and admit that you need help to treat it, there is no possibility of healing it. You can put a bandage over it and let the wound fester underneath and become infected. Or you can choose to admit that you need help to clean it properly so it can truly heal, and in so doing, you can transform your story.

Thankfully healing, peace, and transformation are possible! I know because I found them, as have many other women. My journey to seek healing after my abortion led me to some of the greatest stories ever told. They include stories of love, betrayal, adventure, tears, hope, forgiveness, more love, and transformation. Seeing my story through the lens of these other stories put me on a path to recovery and transformation. Are these the kinds of stories you want to read and maybe relate to your life? These great stories are actually found in the Bible. By reviewing them and exploring how we can relate them to our own lives, we can find hope. We can grieve our loss and find God's love, forgiveness, restoration, and transformation.

Check out how this process works by reading the story of Jesus (who is God) meeting a woman in Samaria, a region north of Judea, in Israel.

### Consider John 4:4–19, 25–26

He [Jesus] had to go through Samaria on the way. Eventually he came to the Samaritan village of Sychar, near the field that Jacob gave to his son Joseph. Jacob's well was there; and Jesus, tired from the long walk, sat wearily beside the well about noontime. Soon a Samaritan woman came to draw water, and Jesus said to her, "Please give me a drink." He was alone at the time because his disciples had gone into the village to buy some food.

[9] The woman was surprised, for Jews refuse to have anything to do with Samaritans. She said to Jesus, "You are a Jew, and I am a Samaritan woman. Why are you asking me for a drink?"

Jesus replied, "If you only knew the gift God has for you and who you are speaking to, you would ask me, and I would give you living water."

"But sir, you don't have a rope or a bucket," she said, "and this well is very deep. Where would you get this living water? And besides, do you think you're greater than our ancestor Jacob, who gave us this well? How can you offer better water than he and his sons and his animals enjoyed?"

Jesus replied, "Anyone who drinks this water will soon become thirsty again. But those who drink the water I give will never be thirsty again. It becomes a fresh, bubbling spring within them, giving them eternal life."

"Please, sir," the woman said, "give me this water! Then I'll never be thirsty again, and I won't have to come here to get water."

"Go and get your husband," Jesus told her.

"I don't have a husband," the woman replied.

Jesus said, "You're right! You don't have a husband—for you have had five husbands, and you aren't even married to the man you're living with now. You certainly spoke the truth!"

"Sir," the woman said, "you must be a prophet."

. . . . The woman said, "I know the Messiah is coming—the one who is called Christ. When he comes, he will explain everything to us."

[26] Then Jesus told her, "I AM the Messiah!"

**Let's Talk**

Verse 9 tells us that Jews did not get along with Samaritans, and Jesus was Jewish. Also, back in the time of this story, men did not typically speak directly to women. So the Samaritan woman was shocked that Jesus would want to speak to her. Have you ever felt like that? That Jesus (God) would not want to talk with you? Why?

Water was very scarce in Samaria, and wells were shared by an entire neighborhood. The women of a town would go to the neighborhood well daily to supply their needs just for the day. Most women went to the well early in the morning, before the heat of the day. Yet this woman waited until noon, after all others were gone. Based on this woman's lifestyle, why do you think she waited? Do you see a similar pattern in your life? In what way?

Jesus offered the woman "living water" to quench her "thirst" forever. Do you think the Samaritan woman understood that Jesus was using water as a symbol for the gift of life He was really offering? What type of thirst do you think she really had? What type of thirst do you want satisfied or healed? What have you sought to quench your thirst? A certain lifestyle, or the affirmation of certain people? Has it worked? Why or why not?

Jesus knew everything about the Samaritan woman: her questionable past and her secret present. Yet He wanted to relate to her and offer her living water of peace and eternal life. Jesus knows your story, too. How does this make you feel? Comforted, anxious, ashamed, at peace? Do you believe Jesus wants to connect with you and give you the peace of healing? If not, what keeps you from believing it?

The Samaritan woman was the first person to learn from Jesus that He was the Messiah (or Savior), in verse 26. Jesus chose to reveal this truth about Himself to a woman of a different culture, an outcast in her society living a difficult life. He chose to offer her the living water of peace and renewal. He knows you and your life circumstances, and He wants to offer that living water to *you*, too! He wants to share truths about Himself with you. The Samaritan woman mattered to Him, and you matter to Him!

### Make It Personal

Just like the woman at the well, you have a choice—to drink (or not) from the "living water" that will quench your thirst and become a bubbling spring of healing. Pour yourself a glass of cool, crisp, clear water and think about your "thirst." As you take a long drink, feel the refreshment of the living, healing water entering into your body, heart, and mind.

*If you are in a group, the facilitator will lead everyone*
*in a modified version of this activity.*

On this path to healing, complete a chapter each week to apply biblical stories such as this one to your own life. This guidebook will carry you down the path for the next eight weeks as you process the layers of emotions and pick up practical tools to aid your progress. There may be bumps and difficulties along the way, just as there are during physical healing. But the destination is so worth it. The freedom, peace, and healing on the other side make for a happier ending than you can imagine!

You may identify with some of the characters you meet along the way in the stories you read. May they all point you to the One character who will bring you peace and healing and transform your story.

My heart and prayers also accompany you on this path!

### Journey Further

Read Psalm 25, which is considered a prayer for help in times of trouble. Prayer is an ideal way to begin.

You have already completed a "Where Are You?" check list. Consider creating a list titled "Where I Want to Be." At times this path may be difficult and tiring, so take good care of yourself and reflect on your list along the way to inspire you to continue.

# SARA

*A Story of Hope*

When I started my track toward healing from my past abortion, I was in a dark, desperate place. I had not heard of or known anyone who had had an abortion. Up to that point in my life, the only thing I had been told about my abortion was that it was for the best. I had believed that I needed to have it done and that my life would be better because of it.

But I didn't feel better at all. I didn't know what was wrong with me. I felt like I had done something terribly wrong and was beyond sad and hurting from it. I sought counseling to deal with this conflict. I had so much anger toward the people who told me it was the best and only choice I had. My counselor referred me to a pregnancy center and told me about how they offer help to women who are struggling with past abortions. That was when my healing began.

On the path to abortion recovery, I was able to understand my feelings. I was able to meet a woman who had had an abortion and felt the same way I did. She had regret and hurt from an abortion as well.

The difference was that she had been through something called healing. Even though she regretted her abortion, she had rid herself of the guilt, shame, and anger that I was still suffering.

This gave me hope. Hope that I wasn't alone in how I felt.

Hope that things could and would get better.

# CHAPTER 1

# REVEAL THE STORY

*There is nothing concealed that will not be disclosed,*
*or hidden that will not be made known.*
—MATTHEW 10:26 (NIV)

*You're blessed when you're at the end of your rope.*
*With less of you there is more of God and his rule.*
—MATTHEW 5:3 (MSG)

By responding to the "Where Are You?" questions in the introduction, you may have made some surprising connections between your behaviors and feelings and your abortion experience. Perhaps you've tried to cope with the pain of your choice in various ways. Maybe you buried it or tried to run from it or cover it up somehow. The truth is that you are powerless to change your past, what you did, or how it has shaped you thus far. You do have choices today, though! You can choose to reveal your story to the One who can and will offer you comfort and hope, so you can learn from and transform how your story impacts you going forward.

## POWERLESSNESS

Review the following story of a young woman's powerlessness and God's response to her. In the time of this story, servanthood was common. Because children, especially heirs, were so highly valued in this society, it was not unusual for an infertile woman to urge her husband to sleep with her maidservant to gain a child. A child conceived between a man and a maidservant would be considered the man's child and an heir to his estate.

### Consider Genesis 16:1–15

Now Sarai, Abram's wife, had not been able to bear children for him. But she had an Egyptian servant named Hagar. So Sarai said to Abram, "The LORD has prevented me from having children. Go and sleep with my servant. Perhaps I can have children through her." And

Abram agreed with Sarai's proposal. So Sarai, Abram's wife, took Hagar the Egyptian servant and gave her to Abram as a wife. . . .

So Abram had sexual relations with Hagar, and she became pregnant. But when Hagar knew she was pregnant, she began to treat her mistress, Sarai, with contempt. Then Sarai said to Abram, "This is all your fault! I put my servant into your arms, but now that she's pregnant she treats me with contempt. The Lord will show who's wrong—you or me!"

Abram replied, "Look, she is your servant, so deal with her as you see fit." Then Sarai treated Hagar so harshly that she finally ran away.

The angel of the Lord found Hagar beside a spring of water in the wilderness, along the road to Shur. The angel said to her, "Hagar, Sarai's servant, where have you come from, and where are you going?"

"I'm running away from my mistress, Sarai," she replied.

The angel of the Lord said to her, "Return to your mistress, and submit to her authority." Then he added, "I will give you more descendants than you can count."

And the angel also said, "You are now pregnant and will give birth to a son. You are to name him Ishmael (which means 'God hears'), for the Lord has heard your cry of distress. . . .

Thereafter, Hagar used another name to refer to the Lord, who had spoken to her. She said, "You are the God who sees me." She also said, "Have I truly seen the One who sees me?" So that well was named Beer-lahai-roi (which means "well of the Living One who sees me"). It can still be found between Kadesh and Bered.

So Hagar gave Abram a son, and Abram named him Ishmael.

### Let's Talk

What do you think Hagar was thinking and feeling about her life and circumstances with Sarai? With Abram?

In what ways do you relate to Hagar's story and feelings? Can you relate to her choice to run?

In Hagar's wilderness despair, God sent an angel to her, who asked her, "Where are you going?" Do you think Hagar knew where she was running? Have you tried to run from your circumstances? Where are you going?

The angel met Hagar where she was and gave her the name Ishmael for her son. What did this reveal about God? After this, Hagar used a new name for the Lord. What do you think this name meant to her?

What are your thoughts about God from this story? Do you think He will meet you where you are?

God knew Hagar's circumstances, her story, and her choice to run. He met her where she was, before she cried out loud, to comfort her and give her hope for her future. She was powerless to change her circumstances and needed courage to go back to them to obtain her promise of many descendants. We are powerless to change our past, and need courage to go back to examine and process our story to obtain healing and recovery. God will meet us there and will see and hear us and give us hope, just as He did for Hagar.

## CHOICES

As we look back at our stories, we begin to face the reality of the choices we made. We are not the only ones who have made choices that led to sadness and perhaps more bad choices in our lives. The Bible tells of many people who made choices that were harmful to others and to themselves. Read the following story of King David, a man whose mistakes cost much, and consider how this relates to your own story.

**Consider 2 Samuel 11:1–27**

In the spring of the year, when kings normally go out to war, David sent Joab and the Israelite army to fight the Ammonites. They destroyed the Ammonite army and laid siege to the city of Rabbah. However, David stayed behind in Jerusalem.

Late one afternoon, after his midday rest, David got out of bed and was walking on the roof of the palace. As he looked out over the city, he noticed a woman of unusual beauty taking a bath. He sent someone to find out who she was, and he was told, "She is Bathsheba, the daughter of Eliam and the wife of Uriah the Hittite." Then David sent messengers to get her; and when she came to the palace, he slept with her. She had just completed the purification rites after having her menstrual period. Then she returned home. Later, when Bathsheba discovered that she was pregnant, she sent David a message, saying, "I'm pregnant."

Then David sent word to Joab: "Send me Uriah the Hittite." So Joab sent him to David. When Uriah arrived, David asked him how Joab and the army were getting along and how the war was progressing. Then he told Uriah, "Go on home and relax." David even sent a gift to Uriah after he had left the palace. But Uriah didn't go home. He slept that night at the palace entrance with the king's palace guard.

When David heard that Uriah had not gone home, he summoned him and asked, "What's the matter? Why didn't you go home last night after being away for so long?"

Uriah replied, "The Ark and the armies of Israel and Judah are living in tents, and Joab and my master's men are camping in the open fields. How could I go home to wine and dine and sleep with my wife? I swear that I would never do such a thing."

"Well, stay here today," David told him, "and tomorrow you may return to the army." So Uriah stayed in Jerusalem that day and the next. Then David invited him to dinner and got him drunk. But even then he couldn't get Uriah to go home to his wife. Again he slept at the palace entrance with the king's palace guard.

So the next morning David wrote a letter to Joab and gave it to Uriah to deliver. The letter instructed Joab, "Station Uriah on the front lines where the battle is fiercest. Then pull back so that he will be killed." So Joab assigned Uriah to a spot close to the city wall where he knew the enemy's strongest men were fighting. And when the enemy soldiers came out of the city to fight, Uriah the Hittite was killed along with several other Israelite soldiers.

Then Joab sent a battle report to David. He told his messenger, "Report all the news of the battle to the king. But he might get angry and ask, 'Why did the troops go so close to the city? Didn't they know there would be shooting from the walls? Wasn't Abimelech son of Gideon killed at Thebez by a woman who threw a millstone down on him from the wall? Why would you get so close to the wall?' Then tell him, 'Uriah the Hittite was killed, too.'"

So the messenger went to Jerusalem and gave a complete report to David. "The enemy came out against us in the open fields," he said. "And as we chased them back to the city gate, the archers on the wall shot arrows at us. Some of the king's men were killed, including Uriah the Hittite."

"Well, tell Joab not to be discouraged," David said. "The sword devours this one today and that one tomorrow! Fight harder next time, and conquer the city!"

When Uriah's wife heard that her husband was dead, she mourned for him. When the period of mourning was over, David sent for her and brought her to the palace, and she became one of his wives. Then she gave birth to a son. But the Lord was displeased with what David had done.

**Let's Talk**

What was David's first decision or choice that led to the rest of the story? Do you think he considered the potential consequences?

What initial decision led you to your abortion? Did you and your partner consider or discuss the potential consequences of this choice?

How do you think Bathsheba was feeling about her role and experience? In what ways can you relate to her, if any?

How do you think David felt about his unplanned pregnancy? David attempted various ways of coping with the pregnancy before choosing to have Uriah killed.

How did you feel about your unplanned pregnancy? What ways did you consider to deal with your pregnancy?

What fears and pressures do you think were relieved for David when Uriah was killed? Do you think he had other emotions?

What fears, pressures, or other emotions prompted you to choose abortion?

David finally found a way to protect his secret. In what ways have you attempted to protect your secret?

## FACING REALITY

We need to face the reality of our secret and realize that our silence keeps us bound to the pain. David also had to face the reality of his secret. Read more of David's story.

**Consider 2 Samuel 12:1–13**

So the LORD sent Nathan the prophet to tell David this story: "There were two men in a certain town. One was rich, and one was poor. The rich man owned a great many sheep and cattle. The poor man owned nothing but one little lamb he had bought. He raised that little lamb, and it grew up with his children. It ate from the man's own plate and drank from his cup. He cuddled it in his arms like a baby daughter. One day a guest arrived at the home of the rich man. But instead of killing an animal from his own flock or herd, he took the poor man's lamb and killed it and prepared it for his guest."

David was furious. "As surely as the LORD lives," he vowed, "any man who would do such a thing deserves to die! He must repay four lambs to the poor man for the one he stole and for having no pity."

Then Nathan said to David, "You are that man! The LORD, the God of Israel, says: I anointed you king of Israel and saved you from the power of Saul. I gave you your master's house and his wives and the kingdoms of Israel and Judah. And if that had not been enough, I would have given you much, much more. Why, then, have you despised the word of the LORD and done this horrible deed? For you have murdered Uriah the Hittite with the sword of the Ammonites and stolen his wife. From this time on, your family will live by the sword because you have despised me by taking Uriah's wife to be your own.

"This is what the LORD says: Because of what you have done, I will cause your own household to rebel against you. I will give your wives to another man before your very eyes, and he will go to bed with them in public view. You did it secretly, but I will make this happen to you openly in the sight of all Israel."

[13] Then David confessed to Nathan, "I have sinned against the LORD."

Nathan replied, "Yes, but the LORD has forgiven you, and you won't die for this sin."

**Let's Talk**

How did David respond when he realized Nathan's story was actually about him and the reality of what he had done?

Thus far, what are you realizing about your own story? How are you responding to this reality?

God knew the choices David had made, yet how did He respond to David's confession (verse 13)?

### SHARING THE STORY

David eventually confessed his secret. Now we have the choice to look back at our stories and share our secrets to find healing. There is a saying "you are only as sick as your secrets," and these secrets have kept us sick in ways we may not have understood. When we stay silent, our minds and bodies respond to the hidden wounds. We share our stories with God so the light of truth can cleanse them, as soap and water can cleanse a physical wound.

**Consider Psalm 32:3–5 (MSG)**

When I kept it all inside, my bones turned to powder, my words became daylong groans.

The pressure never let up; all the juices of my life dried up.

Then I let it all out; I said, "I'll make a clean breast of my failures to GOD."

Suddenly the pressure was gone—my guilt dissolved, my sin disappeared.

**Let's Talk**

What is the result of hiding our wounds and keeping feelings inside rather than turning to God? How have your hidden wounds affected you?

What happens when we "let it all out" to God? Are you hopeful God will give you the same freedom?

Remembering and sharing your story is the first step out of hiding and toward recovery. You need to see memories truthfully to process what happened and find healing.

In addition to sharing our stories with God, we share our stories with each other to know we are not alone and to gain strength from each other. We are encouraged to pray for one another as we continue our journey toward wholeness and healing:

> Make this your common practice: Confess your sins to each other and pray for each other so that you can live together whole and healed.
>
> —James 5:16 (MSG)

**Make It Personal**

Answer the following questions to the best of your ability, using blank paper or your journal. If necessary, review the "Further Questions to Consider" found on page 145 to help you remember important details of your story. Recounting the details here may be difficult, but this step is a necessary part of the healing process.

- Describe your crisis pregnancy experience and how you came to your decision. What were your life circumstances and relationships? How did you feel about the pregnancy and decision? What other options, if any, did you consider?
- Describe the abortion experience. What details do you remember?
- How did you feel physically and emotionally before the abortion? Afterward?
- What changes did you experience emotionally, spiritually, and physically afterward?
- What negative consequences have you experienced since the abortion?

*If you are journeying alone, share your story with a safe support person.*
*If you are in a group, share your story with the group.*

## GOD'S RESPONSE

David chose to confess, and God responded with forgiveness. Read the story of Jesus (God) responding to a man who waited for healing for thirty-eight years next to a pool thought to have healing properties. Some people believed that when the waters of the pool were stirred, they became restorative.

**Consider John 5:1–9 (MSG)**

Soon another Feast came around and Jesus was back in Jerusalem. Near the Sheep Gate in Jerusalem there was a pool, in Hebrew called *Bethesda*, with five alcoves. Hundreds of sick people—blind, crippled, paralyzed—were in these alcoves. One man had been an invalid there for thirty-eight years. When Jesus saw him stretched out by the pool and knew how long he had been there, he said, "Do you want to get well?"

The sick man said, "Sir, when the water is stirred, I don't have anybody to put me in the pool. By the time I get there, somebody else is already in."

Jesus said, "Get up, take your bedroll, start walking." The man was healed on the spot. He picked up his bedroll and walked off.

**Let's Talk**

This man was an invalid for thirty-eight years. How long has your secret kept you paralyzed?

Jesus noticed this man on that day, and asked him a question. Why do you think Jesus asked that? How did the man respond? Why do you think he responded that way?

Jesus sees you today. He asks you the same question: "Do you want to get well?" How do you respond to Him?

Think back to the story of the Samaritan woman at the well in the introduction (see page 11). Jesus knew her life story and her secrets. He brought them to light and offered her living water. God knew David's story and his secrets. He gave David forgiveness once his story was brought to light. Jesus healed the lame man when he confessed his desire to be restored to health. Read another description of God in the Bible.

### Consider Psalm 103:2–5, 8–11 (NCV)

My whole being, praise the LORD and do not forget all his kindnesses.

He forgives all my sins and heals all my diseases. He saves my life from the grave and loads me with love and mercy. He satisfies me with good things and makes me young again, like the eagle. . . .

The LORD shows mercy and is kind. He does not become angry quickly, and he has great love. He will not always accuse us, and he will not be angry forever. He has not punished us as our sins should be punished; he has not repaid us for the evil we have done. As high as the sky is above the earth, so great is his love for those who respect him.

### Let's Talk

What characteristics of God (the Lord) do you see in the above passage? In what way do they help you to believe that God wants to transform your story?

**Make It Personal**

Place a paper mat or symbolic "bedroll" on the floor or on a table. Either kneel on it or place your folded hands on it to pray. Imagine Jesus asking you the question, "Do you want to get well?" Respond to Him as honestly and fully as you can, and then pick up your mat and thank Him for hearing you.

*If you are in a group, the facilitator will lead everyone*
*in a modified version of this activity.*

Healing begins when you acknowledge that you are powerless to change your past or fix the pain that it has brought, and you choose to believe the light of truth can restore you and bring you hope. As you journey on this path, you gain strength from other group members and God and realize that this light gets brighter and you slowly find peace and healing. Will you bring your story to the light so God can provide you with hope for healing and transformation?

### Journey Further

Read Psalm 40 in your Bible. This is considered a prayer for help and reminds us that God cares about us and will rescue us.

# MELISSA

*A Story of Secrecy*

After looking for love in a series of bad relationships, about two months after abortion became legal across the country, I found myself pregnant. It was 1973. I was a senior in high school, seventeen, the oldest of four children in a fairly affluent family, and I had a huge "problem." The father of the child refused to believe the baby was his and completely turned his back on me. When I told my mother, there was no question as to what was expected of me. To this day, I don't believe anyone else in my family knows that I was pregnant and had an abortion.

I went to the local abortion clinic, and they set the appointment for me. No one counseled me or told me what was going to happen.

One Sunday morning a friend, her boyfriend, and I took the train from New Jersey to New York City to a women's center. In that dark clinic, they separated the guys from the girls. They showed the guys what was going to happen. They never showed us (me) what the procedure was.

Ultimately, I found myself on the table in a small room with a nurse and the "doctor." I was told there would be some cramping, but not much. But it was extremely painful. I felt like my insides were being sucked out of me. At one point, I tried to hold the nurse's hand and she literally backed away from me with a look of disgust on her face.

I truly don't remember much after that—just feeling emotionally numb and empty. When I got home, my mom asked me how it went, but when I began to answer her, she said "don't talk too loud, you don't want anyone"—including my father—"to hear you."

The silence began at that moment.

My life spiraled from there. The nightmares and recurring dreams started. As I began to feel again, it was remorse, guilt, shame, and more emptiness. I stuffed those feelings and was very good at that. I very seldom talked about "it" and was very careful whom I talked about "it" to.

I found that even though abortion was legal and supposed to be okay, if you had had one you were looked down upon and judged if anyone found out or if you told the wrong person you had gone through the procedure. I have been called just about every disgusting name there is by guys who found out. They seemed to realize I was vulnerable and they would use me for what they wanted.

My relationships became more edgy, and I was using drugs during the end of my senior year in high school and hanging out with a rough crowd. All my relationships were affected in some way by the abortion. After one particularly difficult relationship, I decided to enlist in the navy and start what I thought would be a new life. But what I didn't realize was that I took my backpack full of rocks with me.

The navy took me to Washington, DC, and I met and married my first husband. After five years of marriage, I was pregnant again, thirteen years after my abortion. This was such a happy time until we found out at the three-month mark that it was an ectopic pregnancy, most likely a consequence of the abortion. Because I had no pain my doctor didn't know what was wrong and sent me for an ultrasound. As the tech put the sensor over my abdomen, I saw my baby in the right fallopian tube. The tech missed it and told me there was no "pregnancy tissue" in my uterus and I wasn't even pregnant.

When I went in for exploratory surgery, I found I wasn't crazy. My baby was in my right fallopian tube and needed to be removed. This baby died, as did my marriage very shortly after the loss of the baby.

I continued to work and get on with my life while grieving. One day as I was walking to work, I tripped and fell, hitting my head hard. As I fell, I remember thinking, "Oh God, I give up!" Eventually I got up from the ground and went home to check my injuries. As I looked at my badly skinned knees, I clearly heard God say to me, "That's what I want you to do with Me. I want you to give up to Me." It was a turning point in my life.

How do I feel today? I can say without a doubt, if I had known then what I know now, I never would have done what I did. I would not have allowed myself to be pressured into aborting my baby. I was never told when I went through the abortion process that I would have to live with this loss for the rest of my life. The shame of getting pregnant unintentionally is nothing compared to the shame of knowing I aborted my baby and caused another baby to not have a chance of living. It was a terrible secret to keep and one that did not allow me to heal completely for as long as I kept it.

But now I am sharing it, and His light has been healing me.

Thank you for the opportunity to tell my story—forty years later.

# JAMIE

*A Story of Brokenness*

I have never experienced more confusion than when I found myself pregnant at twenty years old. "How could this be happening to me?"

Being a follower of Jesus, I did not agree with abortion. Being a college student and not loving the father of the baby, I did not want to have a baby. I was completely torn. I ended up driving an hour to talk with one of my closest friends, and she cried with me. I thought, if I were a little bit older or if it were with someone I loved then I would be willing to handle having a baby, but in this situation I just can't do it. I was still torn and confused but was leaning more toward abortion.

I then went to the father of the baby, Ross (not his real name), to tell him I was pregnant. Hung over and smelling of marijuana, he denied that he could even be the father. I left furious and cried as I drove home, thinking of the mess I was in.

I felt so alone, yet too ashamed to tell anyone else. I searched the Internet for local clinics and to get more information about my options. I found out there was a "less invasive" abortion available because I was so early in my pregnancy. It was a series of pills and did not require surgery. I called the clinic to get more information.

After voicemails from Ross apologizing and wanting to talk, I called him back. I told him what I had learned from the clinic but that I still hadn't decided. He said he would pay for the abortion if I chose that, making sure to stress that it would probably be best for both of our lives if I had the abortion. Then he said, "But if you have the baby, I will be involved. We can get married and do this together." But there was no way I wanted to subject a baby and myself to the care of this man for the rest of our lives. I remember thinking it was a mistake to have told him.

We planned to go through with the abortion a few days later. Having a plan in place didn't stop me from wavering back to the thought of having the baby. I tried to justify the abortion by saying that the baby would be better off in heaven with Jesus than born into a broken family. Deep down I knew it was wrong, but I really didn't see any other way out of this nightmare.

Ross took me to the clinic, and I filled out some paperwork and waited until they called me for an ultrasound to determine how far along I was. I was eligible for the medication abortion and was told the appointment would be six hours long. I couldn't bear having Ross with me that whole time, so I told him to leave and that I would call when I was done so he could pick me up.

The next time my name was called, I went into a room for "counseling." A woman asked if I was sure ending the pregnancy was what I wanted to do. I told her not really, that God views it as wrong, but that I didn't really have any other choice.

She said that right and wrong is not black and white and "all you can do is make the best decision for you in each situation." I asked if my ability to have kids in the future would be affected.

She responded, "While we cannot guarantee anything, since you are having the nonsurgical procedure there is very low risk for harming your body or hurting your chances of bearing children in years to come. What the pills are doing is actually inducing a miscarriage. And because of the series of pills you will take, it is more controlled and better than having a natural miscarriage."

From that point on, the word abortion was never used again. Instead, it was now replaced by induced miscarriage. You wouldn't think that just changing the wording used would make any difference, but it did. Somehow, I felt slightly better about having an induced miscarriage than admitting I was having an abortion.

I remember asking if there were any long-term effects I should know about. The counselor mentioned that a small number of women may have strong feelings of guilt or depression following their abortion if they weren't sure about their decision, but that over time the pain would ease. She reassured me it was not wrong to be here.

I returned to the waiting room and kept reassuring myself, You have no choice. This is what you have to do.

I looked up and saw a girl who partied with some of my friends from college. I tried to avoid her, but inevitably she saw me and came over to talk and was very casual about "getting knocked up." She was almost twenty weeks along and said she was having the abortion because she "didn't want to ruin her body at such a young age." She spoke about having a big volleyball game coming up and she "needed to take care of it before then."

I ended our conversation by telling her I needed to use the restroom. I felt so sick to my stomach. I was judging her for how far along she was and her reasons for ending her pregnancy. But I slowly realized that now, she and I were lumped into the same category of women. Women who have had abortions. I was just like her. And that thought is what made me so sick. No matter what my reasoning or how far along I was, I was doing the same thing to an innocent baby. As much as this encounter upset me, I still felt that I was stuck and had to go through with it. Knowing Ross was my only way home was a reminder of all the reasons I couldn't change my mind.

After a few more hours of waiting, I was called into a room where a nurse went through the steps I would need to follow with the pills. She explained which pills would "terminate the pregnancy" and which ones would "detach the fetus and induce the miscarriage."

Then I waited again for the doctor. They had me take the first set of pills in the office with the doctor present. He even went as far as looking in my mouth to make sure I had swallowed them. He gave me a bottle of pain pills to take for any "mild cramping" I might have, along with his number if I needed anything else.

Ross came to pick me up and we didn't say a word the entire way back home. He asked if I wanted him to stay, and I said no.

I felt numb, but when it was time, I took the last set of pills. It didn't take long for the cramping and pain to start. I took the first dose of pain pills, but the pain only worsened. It was the most painful thing I had ever experienced. I was hunched over on my bed screaming into my pillow, trying to hide it from my roommates. I could hardly breathe. I took more pain pills.

As much as it hurt, I remember thinking, *You deserve this! Look at what you just did.* It felt like I was physically feeling the deep pain my soul was already experiencing.

After an hour or two of the excruciating pain that only seemed to be getting worse, I couldn't take it any longer. I called the doctor and tried my best to make out words between moans. He called in a stronger prescription for me and told me I could not drive to get it because of the other drugs in my system.

The bleeding had started too, and it was much worse than any period I had ever had. I was anxious to get relief from the pain, but the only two people who knew what I was doing were over an hour away. So I had to tell someone else to get the prescription. I called a friend and told her to pick me up at my apartment and I would explain on the way to the pharmacy. After a few failed attempts at getting the words out, I finally managed, "I'm having a miscarriage." She sympathized with me and agreed to not tell our other friends.

The bleeding, cramping, and pain lasted a few days. But that was nothing compared to the psychological and spiritual affects the abortion had on my life. For some time, I just felt numb. I refused to think about it.

My social drinking turned into heavy drinking. I looked for every opportunity to get so drunk I would black out. I was so unstable. I would be at parties with friends having fun and the next minute I was crying in the bathroom alone.

This went on for a few months without my ever linking it to the abortion. I had even started telling myself it was only a miscarriage, as the lady in the clinic called it.

Then my married sister lost her second pregnancy to miscarriage. This was the first time I truly felt the gravity of what I had done. I had killed a baby I didn't want, and my sister had lost one she had already begun to love.

I felt like a heartless monster.

After this my psychological well-being really dissolved. I attached to any guy who showed the smallest amount of interest and was devastated when it didn't work out. I wasn't able to focus on school. I had terrifying dreams about my baby and being a horrible mother. I was angry and snapped at my friends over the smallest things, especially any of those who knew of the abortion, or even those I knew who supported abortion. I started going to church again. I tried getting a new start and forgetting all my mistakes. I tried to mask it all and go through the motions of a normal life.

Shortly after my sister's miscarriage and the death of a friend, I hit bottom. I was driving home from a date and I started to cry. At first the tears were for the friend who had just died, but they didn't stop. I began thinking about my sister, my mom who had died a few years earlier, and then the abortion. I started hyperventilating and couldn't see in front of me. I pulled over into a parking lot. My heart was racing so fast, I thought I was having a heart attack. I called another friend, and she drove to me and took me back to my place.

Once she helped me calm down, I told her everything that was going on in my life . . . except the abortion. I told her I didn't know who I was or how to become the person I wanted to be. I felt broken and "unfixable."

She suggested counseling to help sort out what I was feeling and thinking. I agreed and decided to talk to my dad about helping me afford it. As soon as I saw my dad, I fell into his hug and the tears started again.

After seeing the alarm on his face, I told him, "I just don't understand. I feel like I'm falling apart and I don't know why, or how to stop it." We had an intense, heartfelt conversation that ended with him getting me information for psychological help.

I researched my options, and I spent a lot of time on my knees in prayer, begging God to help me and admitting that I could not make it on my own. I acknowledged that I tried to live the way I wanted to and only made a mess of everything. God wanted me to look up so much sooner, but I refused and wanted to do it my way. I didn't want to sacrifice the "fun" college life to follow Him. If I had only known how much more I would lose by holding tight to my own ways!

But now I am looking up from the bottom of the pit, and He has been answering.

CHAPTER 2

# LIFT THE VEIL

*Then you will know the truth, and the truth will set you free.*
—JOHN 8:32 (NIV)

*You're blessed when you get your inside world—your mind and heart—
put right. Then you can see God in the outside world.*
—MATTHEW 5:8 (MSG)

It took courage to reveal your story, and you may have felt a sense of release as the light of truth touched it. That touch is a great start to prepare you for deeper truth about your thoughts, beliefs, and emotions and the pain of abortion. Without the light of Truth, you hinder your recovery from the pain.

One of the most common tools we first use to deal with a traumatic or distressing experience is denial. Denial is like placing a cloak or veil over the reality of the abortion to keep it hidden in the dark, away from your conscious awareness. The reality is denied to avoid the pain of recognizing how much of your life the abortion has invaded. Exhaustion sets in as you attempt to live life around or past the veiled reality. Emotions and pain grow and become increasingly unmanageable as the reality underneath the veil clamors to be recognized and processed.

Sharing your story allows a peek into the darkness under the veil. As you continue to open up your story and acknowledge the truth of it, the veil is slowly removed so that the light can enter and so that you can learn more about yourself and your relationships as well as experience deeper healing.

**DENIAL**
Denial and other coping strategies are not limited only to abortion. The Bible is full of stories of people who were in denial about various problems. Review a biblical example in Adam and Eve, the first people God created. Notice their actions and God's response.

**Consider Genesis 2:15–17, 3:1–21**

The Lord God placed the man in the Garden of Eden to tend and watch over it. But the Lord God warned him, "You may freely eat the fruit of every tree in the garden—except the tree of the knowledge of good and evil. If you eat its fruit, you are sure to die."

. . . The serpent was the shrewdest of all the wild animals the Lord God had made. One day he asked the woman, "Did God really say you must not eat the fruit from any of the trees in the garden?"

"Of course we may eat fruit from the trees in the garden," the woman replied. "It's only the fruit from the tree in the middle of the garden that we are not allowed to eat. God said, 'You must not eat it or even touch it; if you do, you will die.'"

"You won't die!" the serpent replied to the woman. "God knows that your eyes will be opened as soon as you eat it, and you will be like God, knowing both good and evil."

The woman was convinced. She saw that the tree was beautiful and its fruit looked delicious, and she wanted the wisdom it would give her. So she took some of the fruit and ate it. Then she gave some to her husband, who was with her, and he ate it, too.

At that moment their eyes were opened, and they suddenly felt shame at their nakedness. So they sewed fig leaves together to cover themselves.

When the cool evening breezes were blowing, the man and his wife heard the Lord God walking about in the garden. So they hid from the Lord God among the trees. [9] Then the Lord God called to the man, "Where are you?"

He replied, "I heard you walking in the garden, so I hid. I was afraid because I was naked."

"Who told you that you were naked?" the Lord God asked. "Have you eaten from the tree whose fruit I commanded you not to eat?"

The man replied, "It was the woman you gave me who gave me the fruit, and I ate it."

Then the Lord God asked the woman, "What have you done?"

"The serpent deceived me," she replied. "That's why I ate it."

Then the Lord God said to the serpent, "Because you have done this, you are cursed more than all animals, domestic and wild. You will crawl on your belly, groveling in the dust as long as you live. And I will cause hostility between you and the woman, and between your offspring and her offspring. He will strike your head, and you will strike his heel."

Then he said to the woman, "I will sharpen the pain of your pregnancy, and in pain you will give birth. And you will desire to control your husband, but he will rule over you."

And to the man he said, "Since you listened to your wife and ate from the tree whose fruit I commanded you not to eat, the ground is cursed because of you. All your life you will struggle to scratch a living from it. It will grow thorns and thistles for you, though you will eat of its grains. By the sweat of your brow will you have food to eat until you return to the ground from which you were made. For you were made from dust, and to dust you will return."

Then the man—Adam—named his wife Eve, because she would be the mother of all who live. [21] And the LORD God made clothing from animal skins for Adam and his wife.

**Let's Talk**

What do you think influenced Eve to eat the fruit? What may have motivated her to make that decision? What influenced Adam, given that he was with her?

What factors shaped your decision to have an abortion (finances, circumstances, plans, messages from self or others)? What motivated you?

How did the serpent deceive Eve into her decision? If you believe you were deceived into your decision, in what ways do you feel you were deceived?

Were you encouraged to make the abortion decision, as Eve encouraged Adam to eat the fruit? How? Was there anyone else you encouraged regarding an abortion decision? What are those relationships like now?

Adam and Eve's denial began when they sought to cover themselves and then hid and withdrew from the Lord. How have you tried to cover or hide your abortion secret? Have you withdrawn?

Denial deepened as Adam used blame to cope with his choice to eat. Have you blamed anyone? If so, whom? How has this affected your relationships with people?

Eve rationalized her choice by pointing to the serpent. How have you justified (or excused) your choice?

Life changed for Eve after her decision, bringing consequences of new pain. How did your life change following your abortion?

Why do you think God asked Adam where he was (verse 9)? In what way is God asking you the same question? What is your response?

Although Adam and Eve chose to eat the fruit, how did God care
for them (verse 21)? Do you think He will care for you? If not, why?

In coping with their decision, some women may push pain out of their mind
and manage to act as if everything is okay. Sometimes women may act in unusual
ways contrary to their desires to keep themselves from acknowledging the full
weight of the choice or any related consequences it may have had on themselves or
others. Denial is not meant to be a long-term way of coping with our feelings or
experiences. Prolonged denial only allows our pain to worsen, and perhaps affect
other areas of our lives and relationships.

Think back to the story of King David in chapter 1 (2 Samuel 11:1–12:13,
on pages 20–21). David tried several ways to deny or hide Bathsheba's unplanned
pregnancy. Once he had dealt with the immediate problem, he pushed it down and
acted like it hadn't happened and thought no one knew, until Nathan confronted
him. He was then faced with admitting the results of his choices.

**Let's Talk**
In addition to Uriah, several others were affected by David's
choices. Who else may have been affected by your choices? How?

In what ways have you dealt with or pushed down your secret?
How has this affected you, others, and your relationships with them?

David seemed to be fine until God sent Nathan to confront him with the truth. Did you think you had all the facts when you made your abortion decision? Has time changed your perspective on the facts? In what ways have you been confronted about or by the truth since then? How have you responded?

God wanted Adam and David to see the truth beyond their denial. By learning how we made and coped with our choices, we learn more about ourselves, our coping methods, and how they keep us in denial and prevent us from facing reality.

## DECEIT AND JUSTIFICATION

The serpent that deceived Eve in the story of Adam and Eve is a symbol of the villain in our story, the Enemy of our soul (Genesis 3:1–6). He is a liar and the father of lies (John 8:44). He opposes God and uses deception and manipulation to challenge and misrepresent the truth. He blurs the line between truth and "almost" truth. This causes us to question or distrust God, truth, and ourselves.

Some of the reasons that led to your abortion choice may have been rooted in distortions and lies from the Enemy that have flooded our culture. Believing these lies impacts our decisions, which we learn to justify. To break through denial and find peace, we need to face the reality of these excuses and admit to them.

Some of the justifications we have held on to may have been prompted by fears (of rejection, failure, insecurity), pride (self-interest), helplessness, or other emotions. Some may include statements such as the following: "Millions of women choose it. It is my body and my choice"; "A pregnancy and baby would ruin my plans for my life, so abortion is the right choice"; "Everyone says I have to do it"; "Others will judge me for being pregnant"; and "I can't care for a child right now."

### Consider Proverbs 14:12–13

There is a path before each person that seems right, but it ends in death. Laughter can conceal a heavy heart, but when the laughter ends, the grief remains.

### . . . and Proverbs 29:25 (NIV)

Fear of man will prove to be a snare, but whoever trusts in the Lord is kept safe.

### Let's Talk

What results has the path of choice produced for you thus far? How may your heart be affected?

What or whom did you lean on when you considered your decision? For what reasons did you rely on them?

What is your reaction to the possibility of trusting or relying on God?

Another distortion of truth is calling into question the definitions of life and personhood: "It wasn't a baby yet; it was just tissue or cells"; or "Who knows when life really begins?"

**Consider Psalm 139:13–16**

You [God] made all the delicate, inner parts of my body and knit me together in my mother's womb. Thank you for making me so wonderfully complex! Your workmanship is marvelous—how well I know it. You watched me as I was being formed in utter seclusion, as I was woven together in the dark of the womb. You saw me before I was born. Every day of my life was recorded in your book. Every moment was laid out before a single day had passed.

**. . . and Jeremiah 1:5 (MSG)**

Before I [God] shaped you in the womb, I knew all about you. Before you saw the light of day, I had holy plans for you.

**Let's Talk**

When and how is life created? By whose choice and plans?

Learn about the early stages of human development in the womb by reviewing the "Fetal Development" summary found on page 147. How does this information affect the way you view the beginning of life? If this is new information for you, what is the most surprising thing you learned?

What have you learned about yourself and your view of life that you did not have or consider when you made your decision to abort?

What are your thoughts and feelings now that you have this information?

It is important to note that reviewing this information is not meant to condemn, shame, or judge but rather to help you understand yourself and your circumstances more honestly. Life remains unmanageable as long as only half of the truth is deemed real. While it may be difficult to face certain facts, you take away denial's power to dominate your life, or hem in your story, when you lift the veil and confront the truth. We have to acknowledge the truth (or reality) and seek a power greater than ourselves if we are to find freedom and healing.

## Time for Healing

Once we know and accept the truth about abortion and our responsibility in it—our choices and how we have coped—we can name and grieve the losses it caused. We can connect our pain, thoughts, and behaviors and learn to make new choices. Rather than continue our denial and hide our pain, we can choose to allow God into our story so He can heal us.

Read the story of a woman of faith who was tired of hiding and desperate for healing. In the days of this story, a person who was bleeding was considered by others to be "unclean" or sinful and rejected by God. Anything or anyone the bleeding person touched would also become unclean and rejected. Thus, a woman who was unclean for twelve years was most likely an outcast, unwanted by the rest of society who feared contamination by her.

**Consider Mark 5:25–34**

A woman in the crowd had suffered for twelve years with constant bleeding. She had suffered a great deal from many doctors, and over the years she had spent everything she had to pay them, but she had gotten no better. In fact, she had gotten worse. She had heard about Jesus, so she came up behind him through the crowd and touched his robe. For she thought to herself, "If I can just touch his robe, I will be healed." Immediately the bleeding stopped, and she could feel in her body that she had been healed of her terrible condition.

Jesus realized at once that healing power had gone out from him, so he turned around in the crowd and asked, "Who touched my robe?" His disciples said to him, "Look at this crowd pressing around you. How can you ask, 'Who touched me?'"

But he kept on looking around to see who had done it. Then the frightened woman, trembling at the realization of what had happened to her, came and fell to her knees in front of him and told him what she had done. [34] And he said to her, "Daughter, your faith has made you well. Go in peace. Your suffering is over."

**Let's Talk**

This woman suffered for years, most likely alone, because of her condition. Have you ever felt you have suffered alone because of your choice? How?

This woman spent all her money on doctors, but her condition only got worse. How have you tried to improve your condition since your abortion?

As the disciples or students pointed out, others probably touched Jesus, too. Yet only this woman was healed. Why do you think that is, based on Jesus' statement in verse 34?

The woman was desperate to touch Jesus' robe so she would be healed. If you could touch Jesus' robe, for what would you be desperate? Spend time talking to Jesus about this.

Even though the rest of society shunned this woman, Jesus lovingly gave the woman healing, and told her, "Go in peace. Your suffering is over." Do you believe He desires to do the same for you? Why or why not?

## GOD'S HEART

We've read several stories in which God showed love to, and restored, His people. He provided for Hagar and Adam and Eve, forgave David, and healed the lame man and the woman who was bleeding. God's heart is the same for you. He wants to heal you from the pain you've been experiencing and restore you to wholeness, and He has the power to do so.

> "I have seen what they do, but I will heal them anyway! I will lead them. I will comfort those who mourn, bringing words of praise to their lips. May they have abundant peace, both near and far," says the LORD, who heals them.
>
> —Isaiah 57:18-19

> Ah, Sovereign LORD, you have made the heavens and the earth by your great power and outstretched arm. Nothing is too hard for you.
>
> —Jeremiah 32:17 (NIV)

## YOUR CHOICE

It is your choice to be willing to trust God to heal your story and take this journey. This journey will lead to some intense emotions at times, and will take some work emotionally and spiritually. God desires to set you free, but the Enemy of your soul wants to block your healing and keep you trapped in your pain. He may use different distractions, distortions, and doubts to send you off this healing path. He may

- sidetrack you with busyness or distract you with a flood of thoughts or fears to keep you from God, prayer, or journaling.
- twist truth to discourage you and create doubt (for example, others can be forgiven, but you cannot; you are a disappointment; and you cannot be healed).
- tempt you to just forget it and settle with the pain or use something else to escape the pain temporarily, rather than find real healing from it.

> Stay alert! Watch out for your great enemy, the devil. He prowls around like a roaring lion, looking for someone to devour.
>
> —1 Peter 5:8

**Make It Personal**

The Enemy wants to alienate us from God, and he will distort the truth and whisper lies to us to accomplish that, as he did with Eve. Journal about the following question: What have you believed or understood about God and your relationship with Him? What is God showing you about Himself at this point in your journey? How do you feel about His care for you?

## Plan of Action to Continue

The Bible gives us a great plan of action when the Enemy attacks:

1. Remember the truth that God, Jesus Christ, is powerful and greater than the Enemy and He wants you to have a more abundant life!

   The thief [the Devil] comes only to steal and kill and destroy; I [Jesus] have come that they may have life, and have it to the full.
   —John 10:10 (NIV)

2. Protect your weak spots: those areas in which you face greatest temptation to quit, doubt, escape, or procrastinate.

   Resist the devil, and he will flee from you.
   —James 4:7 (NIV)

   **List the reasons why** you have chosen to complete this study and receive healing. When the Enemy tempts you to quit, review these reasons and tell the Enemy to flee!

3. Pick up the weapon of prayer: Ask God for His help on a daily basis; simply talk to Him about everything you are feeling and thinking.

   "Lord, help!" they cried in their trouble, and he saved them from their distress. He sent out his word and healed them, snatching them from the door of death.
   —Psalm 107:19–20

**A simple prayer is Psalm 31:2:**

Lord, "be my rock of protection, a fortress where I will be safe." Write this on a card and keep it where you will see and speak it often.

4. Remember your support team. Ask them to pick up their weapons and pray for you.

> When a believing person prays, great things happen.
> —James 5:16 (NCV)

Hear Jesus' invitation to join this journey, and consider whether you are willing to take it and share your story with God:

> Are you tired? Worn out? Burned out on religion? Come to me. Get away with me and you'll recover your life. I'll show you how to take a real rest. Walk with me and work with me—watch how I do it. Learn the unforced rhythms of grace. I won't lay anything heavy or ill-fitting on you. Keep company with me and you'll learn to live freely and lightly.
> —Matthew 11:28–30 (MSG)

If you are willing to accept this invitation to continue, you will begin to take inventory of the emotional outcomes of your abortion story in the next chapter. You will continue to learn more of the truth about God as well. At times this emotional journey may be difficult, but if you stay numb emotionally, you won't deal with the things that must be addressed in order to experience healing. Pray and ask God to give you the strength and endurance to continue on this healing path. The destination of a life of peace and joy is worth it!

**Make It Personal**

Imagine Jesus inviting you on a healing getaway to recover your story. He invites you to walk with Him and learn from Him.

*Jesus Christ*
*Requests the honor of your presence on a*

*Healing Getaway*

*To recover your story*
*Walk with Me and learn from Me*
*Learn the unforced rhythms of grace*
*And live freely and lightly*

*The favor of a reply is requested*

Write a note in reply, letting Him know the area in which you desire rest and healing. Consider placing this note in a box or basket, symbolic of a mailbox to God.

*If you are in a group, the facilitator will lead everyone*
*in a modified version of this activity.*

**JOURNEY FURTHER**

Read Psalm 51, a prayer of confession. David wrote this psalm in response to Nathan's confrontation of his sin.

Complete the first "Responsibility and Influence Pie" worksheet, found on page 149. If you are in a group, your completed pie may be discussed in the group. If not, share your pie with your support person.

# ANNETTE

*A Story of Honesty*

My journey to peace did not come without difficulty. One of the hardest things for me was honesty—acknowledging that my abortion choice resulted in the loss of a child.

I experienced extreme levels of anxiety, which was at many times completely debilitating. I learned the anxiety was my body's coping mechanism for dealing with the unresolved feelings I was hiding within. I had successfully erased this choice of abortion from my mind, but my body hadn't erased the memory of the child I had created inside of me.

I could accept the fact that abortion was wrong, but I did not want to accept the fact that this wrongful act had resulted in the loss of a child. I was afraid of acknowledging this because I was afraid of the pain that comes with losing a child. I had accepted the truth of what I had done but I had not yet accepted this fact.

I was afraid of admitting it, and my anxiety was at an all-time high. I could surrender to my anxiety, as I had so many times before, or I could face the fear and deal with my feelings once and for all. I was tired of being a slave to my anxiety, and a small part of me was excited. Excited because it meant there was a reason for my anxiety and that, by the grace of God, through this healing path I had been given the tools I needed to fix it. I was humbled by His love for me, despite all the hurtful things I had done, and I was grateful for His amazing grace in my life.

When I refocused my thoughts on the truth, I was focusing on what is right and good. Focusing on what is right and good removed the negative thoughts from my mind and allowed the light of Jesus to shine through.

I know that as long as I keep my focus on Him I will never lose my way.

# CHAPTER 3

# TAME THE HEAT

*Stop being angry! Turn from your rage!*
*Do not lose your temper—it only leads to harm.*
—PSALM 37:8

*You're blessed when you can show people how to cooperate*
*instead of compete or fight. That's when you discover who you really are,*
*and your place in God's family.*
—MATTHEW 5:9 (MSG)

In the last chapter, you began to see the truth about abortion and the loss of a child it brought. In this chapter and the next, you will start to take inventory of the emotional effects related to this loss. Sometimes after an abortion we can numb our emotions or give them too much control over our lives. An "emotional inventory" is another step toward seeing ourselves and situation more clearly. Begin by examining the emotional response of anger, which is common to any loss.

Anger is a God-given emotion that suggests something may be wrong and needs attention. Whether it is on the surface and we seethe in the heat of it or it has been pushed down and boils underneath like a toxic waste pool, our anger needs to be processed in a healthy way. Anger can be a roadblock to healing if it is not recognized and released.

## TYPES OF ANGER

According to Gary Chapman in his book *Anger: Handling a Powerful Emotion in a Healthy Way*, God gave us anger to "motivate us to take positive, constructive action" to help others and our relationships, or to "seek to set something right" when we encounter injustice or genuine wrongdoing.[5] In other words, anger's expression should be to benefit others, not harm them. Chapman states that when our anger stems from wrongdoing, it is considered *definitive anger*.

Review the following biblical example of Jesus expressing His God-given emotion of anger. At the time of this story, certain items were required to worship at the temple. Jesus went to the temple to pray and saw businessmen cheating the people who came to pray by charging excessive prices for the required items. Those who could not afford to buy the items were not allowed to participate in temple worship. This injustice angered Jesus.

**Consider Matthew 21:12–14 (MSG)**

Jesus went straight to the Temple and threw out everyone who had set up shop, buying and selling. He kicked over the tables of loan sharks and the stalls of dove merchants. He quoted this text:

> My house was designated a house of prayer;
> You have made it a hangout for thieves.

Now there was room for the blind and crippled to get in. They came to Jesus and he healed them.

**Let's Talk**

How did Jesus respond to His anger? In what way was His anger warranted?

Would you say His response was beneficial? How so, or what changes took place as a result?

Jesus' response to His anger was to end injustice and benefit others. His example suggests that our goal is not to eliminate anger but to be aware of what sparked it and to respond to it appropriately and in a controlled manner in order to bring constructive results. Anger is like the warning light on the dashboard of a car, signaling a need for attention. If we ignore it or don't deal with it properly, the car may be damaged. When we disregard anger or express anger destructively, it can be harmful to ourselves and others.

A biblical example of anger that was expressed in a hostile way emerges from a story of betrayal. At the time of this story, Jesus was falsely accused of breaking a Jewish law. The innocent Jesus was betrayed to the authorities for arrest, whose soldiers advanced against Him with swords and clubs.

**Consider Matthew 26:51–52 (MSG)**

Then they [the authorities' soldiers] came on him [Jesus]—grabbed him and roughed him up. One of those with Jesus pulled his sword and, taking a swing at the Chief Priest's servant, cut off his ear. [52] Jesus said, "Put your sword back where it belongs. All who use swords are destroyed by swords."

**Let's Talk**

How did Jesus' follower respond to his anger? Would you say this response was healthy and effective in stopping the unjust arrest?

In what ways may your expression of anger be like a sword?

What about your abortion decision made you angry? How have you dealt with it so far?

Jesus' words in verse 52 remind us that harmful expressions of anger can lead to a cycle of pain and retribution. This is true whether the anger is definitive or what Chapman calls *distorted anger*, which often stems from, or covers up, a loss of control, or stems from other emotions such as hurt, fear, guilt, shame, envy, or embarrassment. The pressure from stifling such emotions can bubble over or burst into anger.

According to Chapman, distorted anger may also arise from "mere disappointment, unfulfilled desire, a frustrated effort, or a bad mood."[6] This may include unmet expectations that others will do, say, or be as we wish. This type of anger does not benefit others and can be misdirected when we take a situation or others' actions personally with a self-serving, selfish focus. Remember, anger is like the warning light on the car dashboard, so it is important to determine the root causes of it, so you can address the underlying problem instead of acting out and causing damage to others or yourself.

We are told the story of a man with distorted anger in the Bible. Naaman was a commander in the army of Aram who had leprosy, a terrible skin disease that had no cure at the time. The Aramean king sent him to God's prophet Elisha in Israel to obtain healing.

### Consider 2 Kings 5:9–14

So Naaman went with his horses and chariots and waited at the door of Elisha's house. But Elisha sent a messenger out to him with this message: "Go and wash yourself seven times in the Jordan River. Then your skin will be restored, and you will be healed of your leprosy."

But Naaman became angry and stalked away. "I thought he would certainly come out to meet me!" he said. "I expected him to wave his hand over the leprosy and call on the name of the Lord his God and heal me! Aren't the rivers of Damascus, the Abana and the Pharpar, better than any of the rivers of Israel? Why shouldn't I wash in them and be healed?" So Naaman turned and went away in a rage.

But his officers tried to reason with him and said, "Sir, if the prophet had told you to do something very difficult, wouldn't you have done it? So you should certainly obey him when he says simply, 'Go and wash and be cured!'" So Naaman went down to the Jordan River and dipped himself seven times, as the man of God had instructed him. And his skin became as healthy as the skin of a young child, and he was healed!

**Let's Talk**

What was the cause of Naaman's anger? How did he express his anger?

Naaman's response to his anger nearly hindered his opportunity to be healed. How has your response to anger hindered your ability to heal?

## Expressing Anger

There are two unhealthy ways of expressing anger: erupting and smoldering. Erupting is outwardly expressing anger in a harsh manner, either verbally or physically. It can include screaming, condemning, bullying, or acts of violence. Erupters often blame others or desire to get revenge.

**Consider Romans 12:19**

Dear friends, never take revenge. Leave that to the righteous anger of God. For the Scriptures say, "I will take revenge; I will pay them back," says the Lord.

**Let's Talk**

Have you blamed others or desired to get even with anyone from your abortion experience? If so, how have you responded to this anger?

Smoldering is storing anger inside. It typically begins with silence and denial. In time, this bottled-up anger leads to withdrawal, resentment, and bitterness. Smoldering anger is like a dormant volcano, with lava bubbling beneath the surface. As hurts are reviewed over and over, the lava turns into hot bitterness inside, burning various areas of your life and leaving you miserable and even emotionally and physically sick (for instance, by leaving you with ulcers, headaches, exhaustion, and depression). The hot lava may slowly seep out in more subtle ways such as negativity, sarcasm, or gossip, or it may erupt without warning at any time and at anyone for an unrelated reason.

**Consider Hebrews 12:15**

Look after each other so that none of you fails to receive the grace of God. Watch out that no poisonous root of bitterness grows up to trouble you, corrupting many.

**Let's Talk**

How have you attempted to cover up, hide, or deny any anger or resentment regarding the abortion? How have you been coping with the lava of bitterness?

Whether anger is definitive or distorted, it needs to be expressed. However, unhealthy expression of anger is harmful. The key is to learn to manage anger in healthy ways. The Bible gives us some ideas about this.

**Consider Ephesians 4:26–27, 31**

And "don't sin by letting anger control you." Don't let the sun go down while you are still angry, for anger gives a foothold to the devil. . . . Get rid of all bitterness, rage, anger, harsh words, and slander, as well as all types of evil behavior.

**Let's Talk**

In what ways may anger have control over you?

For what reason should we not remain angry long, but instead learn to express it correctly?

Anger is a natural human emotion we all experience at times. When the anger warning light is triggered, it needs to be examined to identify the cause behind it. It is important to determine whether other emotions or past circumstances are involved so we may properly respond. Our response to anger can make a difference in our relationships. Sometimes our pent-up, unexpressed anger may emerge in confusing ways, such as screaming for a minor offense at both those you care about and those you don't know, or avoiding people. Our unresolved anger can be a barrier between us and others, damaging our relationships.

**Let's Talk**

How was anger modeled for you? What have you learned about anger as a result?

How do you express your anger? What does your anger look like?

How do others experience and respond to your anger?

What purpose does your anger serve? (Does it protect you, put you in control, numb your pain or sadness, stifle responsibility, or do something else?)

## RELEASING ANGER

Anger does not have to consume or control you; you can choose to express it in healthier ways. You can learn to manage your anger better over time, but it is an ongoing process that takes time and practice. We may not be able to change a situation, but we can change how we respond to it.

Holding on to anger and bitterness is like drinking poison and hoping another person dies. By releasing the emotions of anger, we can set down the poison and learn to forgive. Forgiveness doesn't remove wrongs, but it can free us from the toxic hold they have on us. We'll learn more about that in a later chapter.

**To begin to process your anger,** try this prayer based on Psalm 142:

Lord, I pour out my complaints to You, and I share with You my troubles. You alone know the way I should turn.

We must acknowledge and name the source of the anger and bitterness that has infected our hearts. It is common for women to be angry with some people, groups, or institutions following an abortion. While not everything in the list below will apply to you and your situation, search your heart and try to be as honest with yourself as possible. If your anger is distorted, consider what other emotions may be involved. Are you angry with

- Those who distorted the truth about abortion?
- Those who encouraged abortion?
- Yourself, for having the unplanned pregnancy?
- The father of the baby?
- Parents or other family members?
- The culture, either religious or social?
- Those involved in the abortion itself?

Sometimes we may avoid admitting our anger toward others out of fear of rejection or abandonment. We may feel disloyal acknowledging anger toward those we believe we are to love and honor. We may fear anger because of unhealthy expressions we have witnessed in the past. We may have worked so hard to control our expression of anger that we have even suppressed our conscious awareness of it. Remember, anger is merely the warning light signaling us to note the problem and respond to it properly to avoid damage. It is important to name and confess the anger to God and respond to it in a healthy way in order to find peace.

Healthy ways to express your anger include running or other physical activity, crying, writing or journaling, artwork, or expressing your anger verbally to God or a trusted friend or counselor.

**Review the "Cool the Heat" spiritual tool** found on pages 151–52. Think about how you can apply these steps to help you manage your anger in a more appropriate way now and in the future.

**Make It Personal**

Express your anger through writing. This can be in the form of journaling, poetry, drawing, or writing letters to those involved in your abortion. You can use the list above as a starting point for the recipients of your letters. Use the anger letter template below to write letters that you will *never* send. Express your feelings openly and honestly. The goal is to expose the deepest root of your anger, which may allow other emotions to surface.

Dear _____ ,

I am angry with you for (or because) _____

_____

_____

I felt _____

_____

when _____

_____

This may have been a tough week, but you are making progress on this path! In the next chapter, you will identify and learn more about some emotions that sometimes lie beneath our anger: anxiety, fear, guilt, and shame. As you process these emotions, you move closer to recovery.

### Journey Further

Read Psalm 55, written by David following the betrayal of a friend.

Complete another "Responsibility and Influence Pie" on page 153 if there are any changes from the first one. Review the list of anger sources on page 65 and consider whether any of these should be added to or changed in your pie. If you are in a group, this may be discussed in the group. If not, share your pie with your support person.

# SUE

*A Story of Anger*

The anger chapter challenged me because I had a lot of anger following my abortion, and I thought I deserved to hold on to it, especially toward the boyfriend who got me pregnant. I was angry that he didn't react the way I thought he should when I told him I was pregnant. I let that anger affect every interaction with him. He could do nothing right in my mind, even when he did do nice things.

I was pretty explosive in dealing with my anger, sometimes unleashing it not only on him, but on friends and others. I lost a few friends over it.

In the anger lesson, I came to realize I had anger toward others that I had buried deep inside. As I completed the chapter and listened to others share in the group, I realized that I had been carrying bitterness and anger toward my mom, who never even knew I was pregnant or had an abortion. I blamed her for my fear of telling her about being pregnant and scared. But I didn't think it was okay to be angry with parents, especially when they try to do whatever they can, so I shoved it down and pretended it wasn't there until I couldn't recognize it. I was surprised to realize the anger was there and that it probably affected our relationship.

I cried hard as I wrote my anger letter and shouted it out as I read it in the group and cried some more. It was exhausting but freeing. To be able to get it out of me felt like dumping toxic waste out of my body! I was able to go back to the chapter and review it and learn that I often used anger to feel powerful (so I exploded), and I began to see where my anger was due to unmet expectations (in addition to other things). It wasn't easy, but I learned so much about myself that has been helpful, not just about the abortion, but in other areas of life.

One thing I took away from this is the importance of being honest with yourself about your anger. I didn't understand how much the buried bitterness affected my relationships until I acknowledged the anger and let it out.

Express your anger in one of the healthy ways suggested! You will be amazed at the difference it can make.

CHAPTER 4

# CLIMB OUT OF THE PIT

*He brought them out of darkness and the deepest gloom*
*and broke away their chains. Let them give thanks to the LORD*
*for his unfailing love.*
—PSALM 107:14–15 (NIV 84)

*You're blessed when you're content with just who you are—*
*no more, no less. That's the moment you find yourselves*
*proud owners of everything that can't be bought.*
—MATTHEW 5:5 (MSG)

In the previous chapter, it was noted that distorted anger may cover up other deeply felt emotions such as anxiety, fear, guilt, and shame. These deep emotions, if turned inward, can lead to a pit of depression if they are not processed. In this chapter, continue to inventory each of these emotions so you can bring them to the healing light of truth.

## DEPRESSION

Many women who have had an abortion experience depression stemming from difficulty coping with the aftereffects. Depression can be mild, such as a feeling of numbness or a general disinterest in life. Depression can also be more severe, leading to withdrawal from others and a sense of hopelessness. It can also drain energy, strength, appetite, and even the motivation to live.

Review the following biblical example of anxiety leading to depression. Elijah was a prophet of the Lord God who defeated the many false, lying prophets of evil Queen Jezebel. In her anger over her defeat, Queen Jezebel threatened Elijah.

> **Consider 1 Kings 19:2–6**
>
> So Jezebel sent this message to Elijah: "May the gods strike me and even kill me if by this time tomorrow I have not killed you just as you killed them."

Elijah was afraid and fled for his life. He went to Beersheba, a town in Judah, and he left his servant there. [4] Then he went on alone into the wilderness, traveling all day. He sat down under a solitary broom tree and prayed that he might die. "I have had enough, Lord," he said. "Take my life, for I am no better than my ancestors who have already died."

Then he lay down and slept under the broom tree. But as he was sleeping, an angel touched him and told him, "Get up and eat!" He looked around and there beside his head was some bread baked on hot stones and a jar of water! So he ate and drank and lay down again.

**Let's Talk**

Elijah's anxiety (fear) led him to be depressed. What fears or questions continue to bother you regarding your abortion?

How severe was Elijah's anxiety and depression (verse 4)? In what way can you relate to this feeling?

What was the response to Elijah's cry to the Lord? Do you think the Lord will provide comfort for you?

While it is common to experience some depression after an abortion, if it is so severe that it affects your ability to cope with daily life or takes away your motivation to live, a professional resource may be helpful. See page 155 for more information on symptoms of severe depression as well as information on resources for help.

**A paraphrase of Psalm 23:4** can be a prayer for when you're feeling depressed:

Lord, even though I walk through dark valleys, remind me that I need not fear because You are with me and comfort me.

## GUILT

Guilt is the feeling of regret and sorrow for committing an action that is outside a person's value system (*I did something wrong*).

Review the story of Peter, a man filled with guilt. Peter was one of Jesus' closest disciples, or students. Jesus predicted to Peter that Peter would deny knowing Jesus three times, before a rooster crowed. In his loyalty, Peter promised this would never happen. However, when Jesus was taken by His enemies, Peter indeed betrayed Jesus by denying he even knew Jesus, when Jesus needed his support the most.

**Consider Luke 22:56–62**

A servant girl noticed him [Peter] in the firelight and began staring at him. Finally she said, "This man was one of Jesus' followers!"

But Peter denied it. "Woman," he said, "I don't even know him!"

After a while someone else looked at him and said, "You must be one of them!"

"No, man, I'm not!" Peter retorted.

About an hour later someone else insisted, "This must be one of them, because he is a Galilean, too."

But Peter said, "Man, I don't know what you are talking about." And immediately, while he was still speaking, the rooster crowed.

At that moment the Lord turned and looked at Peter. Suddenly, the Lord's words flashed through Peter's mind: "Before the rooster crows tomorrow morning, you will deny three times that you even know me." And Peter left the courtyard, weeping bitterly.

**Let's Talk**

In what ways do you relate to Peter? How do you relate to his reaction to his guilt?

Guilt can serve as a very healthy nudge for us to deal with a problem or sin that we may have been ignoring or covering up. Unresolved guilt can lead to difficulty in thinking clearly and bring a sense of heaviness or lethargy. Accepting responsibility, confessing the sin, and dealing with the problem are healthy ways to cope with guilt.

King David accepted and confessed his sin with Bathsheba in Psalm 51, which we read at the end of chapter 2 ("Journey Further"). Let's take a look at how David expressed his feelings of guilt in another context.

**Consider Psalm 38:4–10, 17–18, 21–22**

My guilt overwhelms me—it is a burden too heavy to bear.
My wounds fester and stink because of my foolish sins.
I am bent over and racked with pain. All day long I walk around filled with grief.
A raging fever burns within me, and my health is broken.
I am exhausted and completely crushed. My groans come from an anguished heart.
You know what I long for, Lord; you hear my every sigh.
My heart beats wildly, my strength fails, and I am going blind. . . .
I am on the verge of collapse, facing constant pain.
[18] But I confess my sins; I am deeply sorry for what I have done . . .
Do not abandon me, O Lᴏʀᴅ. Do not stand at a distance, my God.
Come quickly to help me, O Lord my savior.

**Let's Talk**

In what ways do you relate to the symptoms of guilt and depression in this psalm?

How does David cope with his guilt (verse 18)? In what ways have you tried to cope with your guilt (for example, by drowning it, deflecting it, or denying it)?

Guilt is like a lighthouse warning us that danger is ahead if we don't change our heart and redirect our current course in life. If we disregard the warning, we can painfully hit the rocky coast we've been ignoring. If we heed the warning, we turn back around to the open waters, safe and ready for new adventures. Read the following letter written by Paul, one of Jesus' followers, to an early church regarding the people's response to a reprimand he had sent them previously.

**Consider 2 Corinthians 7:8–11 (MSG)**

I know I distressed you greatly with my letter. . . . Now I'm glad—not that you were upset, but that you were jarred into turning things around. You let the distress bring you to God, not drive you from him. The result was all gain, no loss.

[10] Distress that drives us to God does that. It turns us around. It gets us back in the way of salvation. We never regret that kind of pain. But those who let distress drive them away from God are full of regrets, end up on a deathbed of regrets.

And now, isn't it wonderful all the ways in which this distress has goaded you closer to God? You're more alive, more concerned, more sensitive, more reverent, more human, more passionate, more responsible. Looked at from any angle, you've come out of this with purity of heart.

**Let's Talk**

What are the two possible options to cope with guilt (distress) in verses 9–10? What are the results of each?

In what ways have guilt and distress led you to regret (for example, addiction or relationship problems)?

In what ways have guilt and distress led you to God? How?

If we allow the guilt of the abortion sin to lead us *to* God—so we accept responsibility and confess to Him—rather than *away* from Him, we can experience transformation and healing.

## SHAME

Shame is a felt sense of unworthiness, embarrassment, or disgrace (*I am wrong*). According to author Cynthia Spell Humbert, shame involves "a deeply felt perception of permanent unacceptability to God, to others, and to self."[7] This leads to an attempt to hide who we believe we are and avoid intimacy due to fear of being known and abandoned.

Recall the story of Adam and Eve from chapter 2 (on pages 40–41). Before they ate the fruit, Adam and Eve had a great relationship with God. Knowing they were accepted and loved, they could be genuine with each other and with God: "Now the man and his wife were both naked, but they felt no shame" (Genesis 2:25).

Once Adam and Eve believed the lies of the Enemy and ate the fruit, shame entered the story of humankind. In their shame, they believed they were unacceptable to God and tried to hide.

**Consider Genesis 3:7–10**

At that moment their eyes were opened, and they suddenly felt shame at their nakedness. So they sewed fig leaves together to cover themselves.

When the cool evening breezes were blowing, the man and his wife heard the Lord God walking about in the garden. So they hid from the Lord God among the trees. Then the Lord God called to the man, "Where are you?"

He replied, "I heard you walking in the garden, so I hid. I was afraid because I was naked."

**Let's Talk**

How did Adam and Eve react to their shame?

How do you relate to these thoughts and feelings following your abortion?

When the hidden shame is exposed to others without our permission, our shame may deepen. Read the story of a woman caught in the act of adultery whose private shame and hidden sins suddenly became very public. In the days of this story, people who committed adultery were punished through stoning, which consisted of two or more people throwing heavy stones at the accused person until he or she died.

### Consider John 8:2–11 (NIV)

At dawn he [Jesus] appeared again in the temple courts, where all the people gathered around him, and he sat down to teach them. The teachers of the law and the Pharisees brought in a woman caught in adultery. They made her stand before the group and said to Jesus, "Teacher, this woman was caught in the act of adultery. In the Law Moses commanded us to stone such women. Now what do you say?" They were using this question as a trap, in order to have a basis for accusing him.

But Jesus bent down and started to write on the ground with his finger. When they kept on questioning him, he straightened up and said to them, "Let any one of you who is without sin be the first to throw a stone at her." Again he stooped down and wrote on the ground.

At this, those who heard began to go away one at a time, the older ones first, until only Jesus was left, with the woman still standing there. Jesus straightened up and asked her, "Woman, where are they? Has no one condemned you?"

"No one, sir," she said.

"Then neither do I condemn you," Jesus declared. "Go now and leave your life of sin."

### Let's Talk

What thoughts can you imagine this woman had about herself when her sins were exposed to the crowd? What do you think she felt or thought when others suggested the punishment she should receive?

How do you relate to these thoughts following your abortion?

How did Jesus respond to her? Do you think He has the same response to you?

We feel shame when our perception of ourselves does not measure up to the way we'd like to be. We feel defective and develop a negative self-image. Our thoughts, emotions, and actions can all be distorted by this negative vision of ourselves. We may condemn ourselves, spiral downward, and avoid relationships for fear of being known, judged, and rejected.

Think back to the Samaritan woman at the well from the introduction (see page 11). We guessed that she went to the well at noon when the people of her community would not be there so she could avoid interacting with them.

**Let's Talk**
What do you think the woman thought about herself that led her to avoid people? How have you felt about yourself? In what ways have you experienced or expressed shame?

Jesus ensured that the woman knew that He knew everything about her lifestyle, yet He wanted to reach out to her anyway. He wanted to offer her living water, remember? Do you believe now that He wants to offer you living water, too? Why or why not?

The condemning messages we tell ourselves become a hammer nailing shame and contempt into our identity. Statements such as *I am worthless, I am a failure, I am unforgivable, I am alone, I am undeserving of love or healing, I am hopeless,* and other similar thoughts are lies that the Enemy, who is also known as our Accuser, tries to get us to believe. He does this to prevent us from being all that God created us to be.

Shame clings to us as long as we continue to hide and believe the lies and accusations of the Enemy. The lies become a stronghold or fortress over us when we accept them as truth. These strongholds distort our view of ourselves and others, warping the real truth of God's image of us and His love for us.

Here's an example of what this type of thinking may look like: The abortion experience evokes emotions and leads to a thought (e.g., *I failed*), which is distorted to become a lie we agree with and believe (*I am a failure*), which becomes a condemning, shame-filled view of ourselves that can affect our interactions with others—that is, a stronghold. We then may make a subconscious commitment to avoid further pain and shame (*I must be perfect and not fail*). In his book *The Soul of Shame*, Curt Thompson states, "Shame is certainly formed in the world of emotion, but it recruits and involves our thinking, imaging, and behaving as well."[8]

Jesus' follower Paul gives us encouragement for defeating these strongholds. We have been given divine weapons such as prayer, truth, and community.

### Consider 2 Corinthians 10:3–5 (NRSV)

Indeed, we live as human beings, but we do not wage war according to human standards; for the weapons of our warfare are not merely human, but they have divine power to destroy strongholds. We destroy arguments and every proud obstacle raised up against the knowledge of God, and we take every thought captive to obey Christ.

**Let's Talk**

What lies about yourself and your relationships have become strongholds? (Examples may include *I'm inadequate, I'm all alone, I must bury my secrets, I deserve to be miserable, no one can understand me, I'm hopeless, I'm nothing more than my abortion.*)

How can you begin to destroy these strongholds?

## Triumph over Shame

To gain victory over strongholds, we release our pain, our shame, and our past to God and destroy the lies of the Enemy. One of our weapons is the truth of God's Word. We must pay attention to our negative thoughts and internal messages, capture the lies and refuse to believe them. As Thompson observes, "We ultimately become what we pay attention to."[9] Thus, we replace the lies and must claim the truth that God's love for us includes His desire to redeem and deliver us!

> Fear not; you will no longer live in shame. Don't be afraid; there is no more disgrace for you. You will no longer remember the shame of your youth and the sorrows of widowhood. For your Creator will be your husband; the Lord of Heaven's Armies is his name! He is your Redeemer, the Holy One of Israel, the God of all the earth.
>
> —Isaiah 54:4–5

**Post a copy of the Truth Scriptures list** from page 81–82 somewhere you will see it often to remind yourself of God's heart for you and the truth about yourself. Consider adding other truths from Scripture that you find meaningful.

Another weapon we have is prayer. Our felt experience of shame is powerful, so pay attention to your feelings and share these with God in prayer. God wants you to come to Him in prayer, asking for His help to demolish the Enemy's strongholds! Focus on God's love and believe His promises to help you.

> I was in trouble, so I called to the LORD.
>     The LORD answered me and set me free.
> I will not be afraid, because the LORD is with me.
>
> —Psalm 118:5–6 (NCV)

**A simple prayer is based loosely on Psalm 34:4:**

I seek You, Lord, and know You will answer me. Thank You that You will deliver me from my fears.

A third weapon we have is community. Whether shame is triggered by a memory, image, thought, or action, share the experience with a safe friend. Rather than hiding in our shame, we must share our struggles and allow ourselves to be known. Bringing our shame to the light with a safe friend or supportive small group shrinks the powerful hold shame has on us, and invites the healing power of Jesus.

> For where two or three gather together as my followers, I [Jesus] am there among them.
>
> —Matthew 18:20

## GOD'S DESIRE

God wants to release you from captivity to strongholds. Hear His heart for you:

> The Spirit of the Sovereign LORD is on me [Isaiah], because the LORD has anointed me to proclaim good news to the poor.
>     He has sent me to bind up the brokenhearted, to proclaim freedom for the captives and release from darkness for the prisoners, to proclaim the year of the LORD's favor and the day of vengeance of our God, to comfort all who mourn, and provide for those who grieve in Zion—to bestow on them a crown of beauty instead of ashes, the oil of joy instead of mourning, and a garment of praise instead of a spirit of despair. They will be called oaks of righteousness, a planting of the LORD for the display of his splendor.

They will rebuild the ancient ruins and restore the places long devastated; they will renew the ruined cities that have been devastated for generations.

—Isaiah 61:1–4 (NIV)

Write the promises above you most want fulfilled (e.g., freedom, comfort, crown of beauty) on a card that you can carry with you to review throughout the day. These positive words are God's desire for you. Thank God for these promises and spend time planting them in your heart, too.

**Make It Personal**

Destroy your stronghold of lies and replace it with a stronghold of truth. Using the Stronghold of Lies worksheet on page 159, write down some of the lies you have heard and thought about yourself that lead to feelings of shame. Symbolically tear down this wall of lies and shame by ripping the worksheet into pieces and throwing it away.

Next, review the list of Scriptures below and reflect on what they say about your worth to God. Create a wall of truth by writing the phrases and verses that speak to you the most on the Stronghold of Truth worksheet on page 161. You can remove this sheet from your guidebook and post it somewhere to give you daily encouragement. Or keep it with you!

**Truth Scriptures**

I am a new creation. (2 Corinthians 5:17)
I am forgiven. (Ephesians 1:6–8)
I am deeply loved by God. (1 John 4:9–10)
I am totally accepted by God. (Colossians 1:21–22)
I am gifted with power, love, and a sound mind. (2 Timothy 1:7)
I am complete. (Colossians 2:9–10)
I am more than a conqueror through Him who loves me. (Romans 8:37)
I am confident. (Philippians 1:6)
I am free. (Romans 6:18, 8:1)
I am capable and can do all things through Christ. (Philippians 4:13)
I am God's masterpiece. (Ephesians 2:10, NLT)
I am sheltered and protected in God. (Colossians 3:3)
I am valuable to God. (1 Corinthians 6:20, Matthew 10:29–31)
I am God's treasure. (1 Peter 2:9–10)
I am dearly loved. (Colossians 3:12)

I am God's delight. (Zephaniah 3:17)

I am the apple of God's eye. (Psalm 17:8, Deuteronomy 32:10)

I am invited to confidently draw near to God. (Ephesians 3:12)

I am a member of God's family. (Romans 10:9–13, 1 John 3:1–3, Ephesians 2:19)

I am welcome in God's presence. (Ephesians 2:18, Hebrews 4:14–16)

I am being transformed. (2 Corinthians 3:18)

I am a friend of God. (John 15:14–15)

I am chosen. (John 15:16)

I am an heir of God. (Romans 8:17)

I am saved by grace as a gift, not because of my performance. (Ephesians 2:8)

I am a temple of the Holy Spirit. (1 Corinthians 6:19–20)

*If you are in a group, the facilitator will lead everyone in a modified version of this activity that may not include these worksheets. If you are reading this book on your own, complete the illustrations at the back and share them with your support person.*

Pray for God to show you His truth about you and His love for you. Begin to read His Word and know it so you can replace the negative statements with the truth of God's Word. As we practice honest vulnerability with God, others, and ourselves, we deepen our awareness of God's grace and healing. As you accept His grace and His love and apply His truth to your mind, strongholds are not so strong and you gain the freedom of truth, forgiveness, and peace.

### JOURNEY FURTHER

Read Psalm 130, a prayer for forgiveness, acceptance, and restoration.

Write about what emotions you have struggled with most since your abortion (anger, shame, depression). Also journal, write poetry, or create art about what you've learned and experienced thus far.

Complete another "Responsibility and Influence Pie" on page 163 if it differs from previous ones based on the understanding you have gained from this chapter. If you are in a group, the pie may be discussed in the group. If not, share your pie with your support person.

# LAUREN

*A Story of Shame*

It was ten years from when I had gotten my abortion to when I started attending the abortion recovery healing group. Those ten years I lived in agony and darkness from the many lies I believed about myself and about what I assumed God thought of me. Shame had to be the new lot that I was to carry in life because of the sin I had committed.

A few weeks into the group, we came to the session on guilt and shame. My facilitator gave us several large LEGO blocks that each had a word of defeat on it, such as *useless, ugly, unworthy, unforgiven,* and so on. As I put the LEGO pieces together one by one to create the stronghold wall structure, I realized those words were how I portrayed myself; I was reading them as if I was looking into a mirror.

As my facilitator was sharing, I realized that I had built that wall of lies day after day, year after year as I was haunted by the decision I had made ten years before. At that point in the lesson, my facilitator asked each of us to break apart the wall of lies and turn the pieces around to rebuild our wall—only this time it was a wall of truth. Each piece now held new hope and new life, with words such as *forgiven, beautiful daughter of God, redeemed, chosen, worthy, loved,* and so on.

This lesson was transformational for me! What I believed and spoke over myself in darkness was terribly destructive, and it was a strong power of shame and guilt. That is not what the Lord desired for me. He says in His Word to speak words of life and truth—that I am His beloved daughter and He has come to forgive and take away all condemnation. Through the power of Christ, I was able to tear down the wall of lies and rebuild a wall of truth and new life. The wall is a symbol of my heart, life, and mind. That lesson was the pivotal point in my healing journey—when I recognized the difference between lies and truth and started nurturing my life in words of truth.

Sisters, I encourage you today that you have the power of Christ in you to tear down the darkness of shame that is trying to strangle healing and abundance in your life. Christ deeply desires to rebuild your story by breaking apart the lies and forever replacing them with truth.

# BRENDA

*A Story of Shame*

The aftermath of my abortion brought some of the darkest and lowest points in my thirty years of life. Some days I can remember that day vividly, and other days that August morning in 2011 is just a blur in my memory.

Once I woke up after the procedure and spent what seemed like an eternity in the recovery room, I made my way to my car. I was not supposed to be driving after the abortion, but I dared not ask anyone to take me to the facility. Once in the car, I took out the ultrasound picture to really look at it. I needed a reminder of them—*them* because they were twin babies.

As I studied every detail of the ultrasound picture, I started sobbing uncontrollably when I realized that my babies were due on my twenty-fourth birthday. I cannot fully articulate what I felt in that moment. Their due date would never come.

After crying in my car for another eternity, or maybe just seconds, I went into auto mode. Day after day after day after that balmy August morning, I was on autopilot. Masking my pain with a superficial smile and drowning out my feelings of anger, guilt, and shame with food, alcohol, and sexual promiscuity.

Oh, and God? He felt light-years away. Even though I grew up in the church and had a relationship with Jesus as my Lord and Savior, after my abortion I hid myself from Him. Or so I thought. I would try and pray here and there and maybe even ask for forgiveness. But I could not forgive myself. I couldn't rid myself of the shame and guilt I felt and that weighed so incredibly heavy on my heart.

After three years and change, the beginning of a new year brought about a shift in me. I knew I could not continue to live the way I was living. While browsing through my church's website, I discovered an abortion recovery group. After going through the group, the pain, guilt, and shame lifted off my heart and my shoulders. The healing process didn't happen overnight. It took weeks and months to work through years of destructive behavior. I had to dig deep inside myself to peel back layers and trust that God would see me through to the other side of my pain. I had to forgive others that were part of my abortion story and forgive myself.

Receiving forgiveness and living in forgiveness meant choosing to shake off the shame and to live guilt-free. I believed I was forgiven, just as God had forgiven me and separated my sins from me "as far as the east is from the west" (Psalm 103:12). I believed my babies were in heaven, laughing, playing, and running around with our Heavenly Father. I believed I could go on with life unashamed, free, and loved.

CHAPTER 5

# SURRENDER TO GRACE

*But He has said to me, "My grace is sufficient for you [My lovingkindness*
*and My mercy are more than enough—always available—regardless*
*of the situation]; for [My] power is being perfected [and is completed*
*and shows itself most effectively] in [your] weakness."*
—2 CORINTHIANS 12:9 (AMP)


*You're blessed when you've worked up a good appetite for God.*
*He's food and drink in the best meal you'll ever eat.*
—MATTHEW 5:6 (MSG)


You've come so far on this path to recovery! Now that you have recognized the truth and your part in the abortion, identified the lava rocks of anger that need to be removed from your path, and crawled out of the valley of guilt and shame, it's time to soar on the wings of God's grace!

## GRACE

Grace is the undeserved love and favor of God. Grace means that no mistake we make in life excludes us from God's unfailing love. It is a gift from God that means no person is beyond renewal. According to Cynthia Spell Humbert, "restoration can only come through understanding and accepting the healing unconditional love and grace of God."[10] This is certainly true for our abortion stories.

One example of God's grace and restoration is seen through the story of Peter that we began in the previous chapter. Peter wept when the rooster crowed and he realized his sin of not helping Jesus in His greatest time of need, and denying even knowing his teacher! Yet despite this betrayal, despite Peter's abandonment, Jesus later offered Peter grace. In His discussion with Peter, Jesus uses the terms *lamb* and *sheep* as symbols for us, His people.

**Consider John 21:15–17, 19**

After breakfast Jesus asked Simon Peter, "Simon son of John, do you love me more than these?"

"Yes, Lord," Peter replied, "you know I love you."

"Then feed my lambs," Jesus told him.

Jesus repeated the question: "Simon son of John, do you love me?"

"Yes, Lord," Peter said, "you know I love you."

"Then take care of my sheep," Jesus said.

A third time he asked him, "Simon son of John, do you love me?"

Peter was hurt that Jesus asked the question a third time. He said, "Lord, you know everything. You know that I love you."

Jesus said, "Then feed my sheep." . . . Then Jesus told him, "Follow me."

**Let's Talk**

How has Jesus given you an opportunity to show sorrow over your abortion?

Do you think Jesus desires to extend grace to you? Can you hear Him say to you "Follow me"? If not, why not?

Jesus gives Peter an opportunity to reverse his initial denial, a chance to show sorrow over his sin by stating his love for Jesus. Then Jesus asks Peter to not only follow Him, but to also participate in His work by caring for Jesus' people! Jesus offered Peter grace—undeserved favor—and redeemed him. Peter later became a pillar of Jesus' church and a leader of Jesus' followers.

Recall the story of the adulterous woman from the last chapter (see page 76). The crowd was ready to stone her for her mistakes, but Jesus offered her unconditional love and grace.

**Consider John 8:7–11 (NIV)**

When they kept on questioning him, he straightened up and said to them, "If any one of you is without sin, let him be the first to throw a stone at her." Again he stooped down and wrote on the ground.

At this, those who heard began to go away one at a time, the older ones first, until only Jesus was left, with the woman still standing there. Jesus straightened up and asked her, "Woman, where are they? Has no one condemned you?"

"No one, sir," she said.

"Then neither do I condemn you," Jesus declared. "Go now and leave your life of sin."

**Let's Talk**

Why do you think the accusers left when Jesus invited the sinless to cast stones?

Imagine this scene fully, with yourself as the accused woman. Read the verses above aloud, using your name for woman. What is your reaction to Jesus' statement to you?

## CHANGE

Notice that Jesus told the woman to "leave your life of sin." God loves us so much that He doesn't want us to harm ourselves further with the pain and consequences of sin. He wants us to change our ways—to repent. Repentance is acknowledging that, not only did our sin hurt us, it also hurt or grieved God. It is feeling so sorrowful over what we've done that we desire to change our life for the better. It is a humble change of heart and mind, producing a change in behavior. When we choose to turn away from our old ways and turn to God, He has mercy and forgives.

### Consider Isaiah 55:7

Let the wicked change their ways and banish the very thought of doing wrong. Let them turn to the Lord that he may have mercy on them. Yes, turn to our God, for he will forgive generously.

### Let's Talk

In our sin, we hide or turn away from God, yet what does this verse suggest we do? If you have not yet turned to God, take time now to consider what may be blocking you, and then talk with God about it. How will God respond? Our sin is not a barrier for Him.

The Enemy wants us to believe the lie that our sins are unforgivable. When we focus on the feelings and not the facts, we remain trapped by the Enemy's condemnation of us. Remember to tear down the lies and replace them with truth, which is fact. We can rest in His saving grace and find strength when we trust in Him.

### Consider Isaiah 30:15 (NIV)

This is what the Sovereign Lord, the Holy One of Israel, says: "In repentance and rest is your salvation, in quietness and trust is your strength."

### Let's Talk

If you have repented, do you still *feel* guilty? What facts or truth can you rest in instead? Think of the Scriptures and stories in previous chapters.

## RESTORATION

In the previous chapter, we learned the importance of confessing our sin with humility as a healthy response to guilt. This is a step toward healing and restoration. Read the following story and look at the father's (that is, God's) heart for the son (us). What an example of confession, forgiveness, and restoration this story is!

### Consider Luke 15:11–24

To illustrate the point further, Jesus told them this story: "A man had two sons. The younger son told his father, 'I want my share of your estate now before you die.' So his father agreed to divide his wealth between his sons.

"A few days later this younger son packed all his belongings and moved to a distant land, and there he wasted all his money in wild living. About the time his money ran out, a great famine swept over the land, and he began to starve. He persuaded a local farmer to hire him, and the man sent him into his fields to feed the pigs. The young man became so hungry that even the pods he was feeding the pigs looked good to him. But no one gave him anything.

"When he finally came to his senses, he said to himself, 'At home even the hired servants have food enough to spare, and here I am dying of hunger! I will go home to my father and say, "Father, I have sinned against both heaven and you, and I am no longer worthy of being called your son. Please take me on as a hired servant."'

"So he returned home to his father. And while he was still a long way off, his father saw him coming. Filled with love and compassion, he ran to his son, embraced him, and kissed him. His son said to him, 'Father, I have sinned against both heaven and you, and I am no longer worthy of being called your son.'

"But his father said to the servants, 'Quick! Bring the finest robe in the house and put it on him. Get a ring for his finger and sandals for his feet. And kill the calf we have been fattening. We must celebrate with a feast, for this son of mine was dead and has now returned to life. He was lost, but now he is found.' So the party began."

**Let's Talk**

What are your thoughts about what the son did with the father's gift?

What motivated the son to return to his father? What was he prepared to say to his father?

What motivated you to seek healing?

In what ways do you identify with the son in this story?

When the son returned, how did the father respond? What characteristics do you see in this father, who represents God?

Before the son could ask to be a servant, what did the father do? In the time of this story, a signet ring was a symbol of a person's position or authority in a family. What do you think God wants to do for you?

God's forgiveness and grace are available for us to accept, as the father's were for his son. When we humbly acknowledge who we are and who God is and surrender to our need for Him, we open ourselves to receive His celebration of grace.

Remember earlier that Jesus used the term *sheep* to symbolize His people. He also referred to Himself as our shepherd, our caretaker. Read the following story and look for God's delight to restore us (His sheep) as we repent after we stray.

### Consider Luke 15:3–7

So Jesus told them this story: "If a man has a hundred sheep and one of them gets lost, what will he do? Won't he leave the ninety-nine others in the wilderness and go to search for the one that is lost until he finds it? And when he has found it, he will joyfully carry it home on his shoulders. When he arrives, he will call together his friends and neighbors, saying, 'Rejoice with me because I have found my lost sheep.' In the same way, there is more joy in heaven over one lost sinner who repents and returns to God than over ninety-nine others who are righteous and haven't strayed away!"

**Let's Talk**

In what way have you felt like a lost sheep?

What are your thoughts and feelings about God searching for you? How does it feel to know that, when you return, there is much joy?

## GOD'S EXTRAVAGANT GIFT

God's grace is a free gift to us. God's extravagant mercy and grace cost Him the great price of His only Son, Jesus Christ.

> God showed how much he loved us by sending his one and only Son into the world so that we might have eternal life through him. This is real love—not that we loved God, but that he loved us and sent his Son as a sacrifice to take away our sins.
>
> —1 John 4:9-10

Jesus suffered and died on the cross to take on the punishment for all of our sins so that we may be forgiven. The pain, shame, and struggles we had as a result of our abortion were the natural consequences of our choice, not punishment. We may also receive discipline or correction to keep us from continuing in painful sin. Because of Jesus' sacrifice, we are not punished for our sin of abortion, but we may experience consequences.

> But it was our sins that did that to him [Jesus], that ripped and tore and crushed him—*our sins!* He took the punishment, and that made us whole. Through his bruises we get healed. We're all like sheep who've wandered off and gotten lost. We've all done our own thing, gone our

own way. And GOD has piled all our sins, everything we've done wrong, on him, on him.

—Isaiah 53:5-6 (MSG)

By taking all of our sin on Himself, Jesus became our substitute. This means God no longer sees our sin, and the connection between us and God is restored. When we believe that Jesus died for us, for the forgiveness of our sins, and we confess and turn away from our sin, God judges us rightly through His mercy.

Everyone has sinned and fallen short of God's glorious standard, and all need to be made right with God by his grace, which is a free gift. They need to be made free from sin through Jesus Christ. God sent him to die in our place to take away our sins. We receive forgiveness through faith in the blood of Jesus' death. This showed that God always does what is right and fair, as in the past when he was patient and did not punish people for their sins. And God gave Jesus to show today that he does what is right. God did this so he could judge rightly and so he could make right any person who has faith in Jesus.

—Romans 3:23-26 (NCV)

**Make It Personal**
Create a timeline using the template introduced on page 165. Prayerfully plot major positive and negative life events (e.g., relocations, deaths, births, marriages, divorces, key conflicts, traumatic circumstances). Take your time working on it. As you review it, note areas and patterns that have shaped you as well as God's movements of grace in your life. Recognizing the threads of God's kindness can strengthen your confidence in His care for you today and in the future.

## OBSTACLES

Sometimes women who have had an abortion have difficulty receiving and accepting God's free gift of grace and forgiveness. Some hold on to their shame, bitterness, and pain with a tight fist, fearful of what letting go may mean. God's grace and forgiveness pour down, but the clenched hand cannot take hold of it. It is by letting go that the hand is open to receiving the sweet gift God longs to give.

**Here's a simple prayer, based on Nehemiah 9:17:**

Lord, help me to let go of the things to which I cling. Thank You for being a God of forgiveness, gracious and merciful. May I take hold of Your unfailing love.

Some women struggle with the concept of God's grace, believing they have to do something special to earn their forgiveness. God's free gift does not require us to make up for what we've done by becoming superwomen or supermoms. We simply trust that we are forgiven and accept this gift so graciously given to us.

### Consider Romans 11:6

And since it [God's acceptance] is through God's kindness, then it is not by their good works. For in that case, God's grace would not be what it really is—free and undeserved.

### Let's Talk

Like the son in the previous story, do you think you can only be forgiven and accepted if you earn it as a "servant"?

In what ways have you tried to work for your forgiveness?

Re-read Romans 3:23–26 on page 95. How are our sins forgiven?

Have you accepted the need for and sought after God's forgiveness? What conversation do you need to have with Him about your faith in order to receive it?

Some women confuse earthly parenting models with God and expect God to act the same way. We learn much from our parents and people of influence during our childhood. Sometimes we imagine God as being like these people in our lives and expect God to react the way others do. But God is not like people:

> God is not a human being, and he will not lie. He is not a human, and he does not change his mind. What he says he will do, he does. What he promises, he makes come true.
>
> —Numbers 23:19 (NCV)

**Review the "Who Is God?" list** found on page 169 and consider how these characteristics may differ from those of influential people in your life. Journal your thoughts on this. Meditating on God's love for ten to fifteen minutes a day can decrease anxiety and fear and open the heart to receiving grace.

**Consider Isaiah 1:18**

"Come now, let's settle this," says the LORD. "Though your sins are like scarlet, I will make them as white as snow. Though they are red like crimson, I will make them as white as wool."

**Let's Talk**

What does God promise to do for those who come to Him? White represents forgiveness and the removal of stain or blemish. What are your thoughts on settling your sin with the Lord?

## GOD'S GRACE

Can you believe in God's character and Word and say "I am forgiven"? In her book *Forgiven and Set Free*, Linda Cochrane suggests the practice of reciting Scripture aloud but changing the pronouns in the passage to personalize it. Try paraphrasing the following verses from Psalm 103 to begin with "I am forgiven because . . ." and replace *us*, *we*, and *our* with *me*, *I*, and *my* to deepen your belief in His forgiveness: [11]

> He [God] does not punish us for all our sins; he does not deal harshly with us, as we deserve.
> For his unfailing love toward those who fear him is as great as the height of the heavens above the earth.
> He has removed our sins as far from us as the east is from the west.
>
> —Psalm 103:10–12

**Make It Personal**

Consider giving yourself a small gift or tangible reminder of God's grace and forgiveness for you. Perhaps a ring or robe can remind you of the forgiven prodigal. You can write a simple "Your sins are forgiven" (Luke 7:48) card and place it in a visible location. In ancient times, God's people built altars of stone as reminders of God's grace. You can write "Neither do I condemn you" (John 8:11) on a smooth stone—or build your own reminder with any materials.

*If you are in a group, the facilitator will lead everyone*
*in a modified version of this activity.*

Nothing is too big to be excluded from God's love, grace, and forgiveness. No matter what obstacles we stubbornly try to cling to, His grace is there and is sufficient to cover it all. Once you understand and accept God's grace and forgiveness for your sins, you can extend forgiveness to others and to yourself. There is more about that in the next chapter.

JOURNEY FURTHER

Read Psalm 32 to remind you that there is nothing to hide from God. You can share your heart and joyfully accept His forgiveness!

# CAROLINA

*A Story of Grace*

The most difficult part for me on the path to recovery was facing God, because I realized I had done so many wrong things. It was not because I don't know Him. But to know that He loves me and He forgives me, even though I did something wrong—I just wanted to hide from Him, grabbing my face with my two hands. I did not want to be in His presence because I can't explain why I had the abortions. That was the hardest part for me. It was a process.

Now I have accepted His forgiveness, and now I am able to pray. What has changed is not only coming to know Him better, but knowing myself better through this path. Accepting that I am a sinner and not perfect, I understand my nature now, and I know that even if I have a good and deep relationship with God, I am still a sinner. He is the only one who never fails. I accepted His forgiveness because of His love, His faithfulness in my life. I experienced changes. I know it is not because of me—it is about Him, and it is all through Him.

I experienced how He cares for me when I realized that God had been working, nudging me, sending people in my way before healing. He was faithful with provision and relationships with people. He sent people to love me.

He knows everything about me. It won't take one thing more or less for Him to love me more or less. He loves me anyway. I was ready to confess publicly to the group that I accepted forgiveness.

We all are different. God treats us all differently. Seek Him, and He will continue your growth. First, surrender to God. If you keep fighting with God, He cannot do it. Surrender your control of your life, and let Him in.

I needed to let go little by little . . . and I still am.

# JACQUELINE

*A Story of God's Sufficient Grace*

It had been decades since my abortions happened. The acts clearly had been buried deep, away from my consciousness, although the memory could arise just by hearing the word abortion (which I avoided hearing). I was so stuck in the shame, hiding from my own self and others. My deep dark secret had me isolated for all those decades. The art of keeping it hidden had been an art I didn't even realize I'd mastered. I was still a prisoner and didn't even see it until Jesus unlocked the door of shame through my abortion recovery journey. Our wonderful God knew the right time to draw me to the place of His loving healing arms. I had no idea what was about to take place.

I still remember the steps that led up to me becoming a participant. It was a day like any other day, but I clearly remember where I was and what day it was. I was at a special event at church, and God worked on my heart through the speaker. It was time for me to walk along with Jesus and learn about His radical healing love. In my healing group, I could talk about my abortions—and the condemnation that I thought would come didn't. Instead, I received love, acceptance, and healing from it all. Everything that even led me to the point of making the wrong choices was being healed.

It wasn't an easy journey, but I was determined to walk with God on this journey. Never had I been able to experience such depths of His love because of fear that plagued me. But I was not alone, and even when I was afraid, He assured me that He was with me on this journey of Love. It was amazing! I was shedding so much shame and guilt for this decision and other wrong choices.

God's love, grace, and forgiveness were so profound and powerful that I realized He wanted me to come out from hiding. The shame and guilt slowly fell off. Ultimately, I could not hide or live in shame any longer. It was now time to mourn properly and connect with my unborn children. This opportunity was due to the grace of God and the wonderful servants He uses. What a heavy burden I shouldered for so long until God came alongside me to share it and then remove it. His grace was sufficient then and still is now.

Ultimately, we walked this healing path together! God gave me the strength to complete the journey, although it is not fully completed. I gained the tools that were available to me to continue the journey on my own. Some of those tools are seeking out safe friends to confess to and connecting with God through His Word and prayer. My unborn children are now acknowledged as a part of my family and no longer need to be hidden under my shame and guilt.

CHAPTER 6

# RELEASE OTHERS—AND YOURSELF

*But when you are praying, first forgive anyone*
*you are holding a grudge against, so that your Father*
*in heaven will forgive your sins, too.*
—MARK 11:25

*They are blessed who show mercy to others,*
*for God will show mercy to them.*
—MATTHEW 5:7 (NCV)

Forgiveness is the crucial key to releasing the chains of hurt and moving toward freedom. This includes forgiving others and yourself and receiving forgiveness from God. Forgiveness involves facing your feelings and dealing with them honestly. Throughout this guidebook, you've had the opportunity to recognize your anger, hurt, guilt, and shame. Forgiveness is acknowledging the reality of your pain. Forgiveness does not excuse the actions that brought the pain, but it does break the powerful hold it has on you.

## PAYING THE DEBT

The Bible is full of stories that can teach us much about forgiveness and mercy. Read the following story about a servant who was granted forgiveness, but was unwilling to give it to others. At the time of this story, those who could not pay a debt were often thrown into debtors' prison until the family could pay the debt.

> **Consider Matthew 18:21–35**
>
> Then Peter came to him [Jesus] and asked, "Lord, how often should I forgive someone who sins against me? Seven times?"
>
> "No, not seven times," Jesus replied, "but seventy times seven!
>
> "Therefore, the Kingdom of Heaven can be compared to a king who decided to bring his accounts up to date with servants who had borrowed money from him. In the process, one of his debtors was brought in who owed him millions of dollars. He couldn't pay, so his

master ordered that he be sold—along with his wife, his children, and everything he owned—to pay the debt.

"But the man fell down before his master and begged him, 'Please, be patient with me, and I will pay it all.' Then his master was filled with pity for him, and he released him and forgave his debt.

"But when the man left the king, he went to a fellow servant who owed him a few thousand dollars. He grabbed him by the throat and demanded instant payment.

"His fellow servant fell down before him and begged for a little more time. 'Be patient with me, and I will pay it,' he pleaded. But his creditor wouldn't wait. He had the man arrested and put in prison until the debt could be paid in full.

"When some of the other servants saw this, they were very upset. They went to the king and told him everything that had happened. Then the king called in the man he had forgiven and said, 'You evil servant! I forgave you that tremendous debt because you pleaded with me. Shouldn't you have mercy on your fellow servant, just as I had mercy on you?' Then the angry king sent the man to prison to be tortured until he had paid his entire debt.

"That's what my heavenly Father will do to you if you refuse to forgive your brothers and sisters from your heart."

**Let's Talk**

From what debt has God (the king) forgiven you?

Who are your fellow servants you've not forgiven? Consider those individuals whom you listed in your "Responsibility and Influence Pies." What debt do they still owe you?

Are some more difficult to forgive than others? Why?

Forgiving someone can be a difficult thing to do, especially if the person does not say he is sorry. Sometimes there seem to be barriers to forgiveness. Cochrane indicates that this may include the conditions we may set on granting forgiveness.[12]

**Let's Talk**

What conditions do you have in order to forgive? Consider finishing the following statement to help you determine conditions: "I will forgive _____ if _____."

There may be other hindrances to forgiveness. Some may feel more powerful holding on to anger or are unsure or fearful of what forgiveness may mean or allow. Reviewing the fundamentals of forgiveness may help you take steps forward in the process.

## FUNDAMENTALS OF FORGIVENESS

Forgiveness is a powerful step in healing. It is important to understand the fundamentals of forgiveness in order to become open to the possibilities of transformation. The first requirement is to recognize that forgiveness is a *choice*, not an emotion or feeling. It is a decision, an act of the will. We are the ones who determine whether we are willing to forgive. We must take the inner action of forgiveness in order to be freed from the grip that wrongs and resentments have over us.

Here is a summary of some further considerations commonly found in the literature on forgiveness:[13]

- Forgiveness does not mean forgetting. (Memories may remain, but choosing to forgive lessens their destructive power over you.)
- Forgiveness does not mean minimizing the hurt or excusing the actions. (You may forgive someone, but you are not agreeing with what he or she did.)
- Forgiveness does not mean that a door is left open for further offense. (You do not have to trust that person again or accept more hurt.)
- Forgiveness does not necessarily mean resolution or reconciliation. (Reconciliation implies a restoration of trust or friendship.)
- Forgiving someone does not necessarily mean you should contact the offender. In fact, it may be best to not contact someone if doing so could cause harm to yourself or others.*
- Forgiveness means breaking the power of pain, anger, and blame. (Our forgiveness can loosen the grip the wrongdoer has over us. In releasing others from their guilt, we release ourselves from toxic bitterness and hurt.)
- Forgiveness is a process, rooted in God's Word. (It takes time for our inner wounds to heal, just as it would for physical wounds. When we consistently choose to forgive, the person and situation slowly lose their powerful sting.)
- Forgiveness is an act of grace and humility, reflecting the character of God. (When we forgive, we enable God's healing power, and we free ourselves to live and grow in God's abundant grace and love.)
- Forgiveness means giving up our right to hold on to wrongs and resentments.

## Toxic Unforgiveness

Forgiving others heals us from the poisonous toxins of bitterness we carried. Ongoing resentment is one type of unforgiveness. We replay a negative scene or hurt over and over in our minds and hearts, remembering our pain. This is like drinking the toxic poison of bitterness one slow sip at a time, ensuring the toxicity never fades. We can choose to set down the poison, and release others from our unforgiveness. When we do this, we release ourselves. Our willingness to give the

---

* Before contacting someone who was involved with your abortion, consider your true intentions in contacting him or her, what positive outcome or potential emotional or spiritual harm could result from contacting him or her, and how you may be affected by the person's response. Sometimes praying for a person is the best way of granting forgiveness.

gift of forgiveness to others and ourselves opens us to receive the gift of deeper healing from God. Jesus shared the following thoughts on this:

### Consider Luke 6:36–38 (NCV)

Show mercy, just as your Father shows mercy. Don't judge others, and you will not be judged. Don't accuse others of being guilty, and you will not be accused of being guilty. Forgive, and you will be forgiven. Give, and you will receive. You will be given much. Pressed down, shaken together, and running over, it will spill into your lap. The way you give to others is the way God will give to you.

### Let's Talk

What motivation are we given to have mercy and forgive?

Consider the conditions you listed earlier regarding forgiveness. How do you think removing these and granting forgiveness may benefit you?

## FORGIVENESS

Jesus' follower Paul shared the thoughts below regarding our part in the process of forgiveness.

### Consider Colossians 3:12–14

Since God chose you to be the holy people he loves, you must clothe yourselves with tenderhearted mercy, kindness, humility, gentleness, and patience. Make allowance for each other's faults, and forgive anyone who offends you. Remember, the Lord forgave you, so you must forgive others. Above all, clothe yourselves with love, which binds us all together in perfect harmony.

**Let's Talk**

What conditions, if any, are given here as to who and why we are to forgive?

Imagine these characteristics as articles of clothing you put on. Are some articles uncomfortable to wear? In what way?

How do your conditions or obstacles "fit" when this clothing is on?

## THE TOOLS GOD GIVES US

When we forgive, we "let go and let God" by releasing the person into God's hands and allowing God to hold him or her accountable. We trust that God will deal with the person in His timing, in His way, recognizing His character of justice. In her book *Praying God's Word*, Beth Moore suggests that forgiveness comes easier when we learn to pray *about* the person and *for* the person.[14]

Praying *about* the person is acknowledging the anger and hurt and pouring your heart out to God about your pain.

> I cry out to the LORD; I plead for the LORD's mercy. I pour out my complaints before him and tell him all my troubles.
>
> —Psalm 142:1-2

Admitting our feelings and pouring out the bitterness to God out loud allows His cleansing light to shine on it, rather than letting it fester in the darkness of our minds and hearts.

Praying *for* the person who hurt or angered us opens us up to the blessing of freedom from the poison of bitterness.

> Don't repay evil for evil. Don't retaliate with insults when people insult you. Instead, pay them back with a blessing. That is what God has called you to do, and he will grant you his blessing.
>
> —1 Peter 3:9

> Bless those who curse you. Pray for those who hurt you.
>
> —Luke 6:28

Choosing to forgive and pray for God to bless those who have hurt us requires humility and a consistent commitment, often on a daily basis. Over time, the freedom of forgiveness settles into our hearts as we mirror God's forgiveness of us.

---

**A simple prayer may be**

Lord, bless _____, and change my heart.

---

## MERCY AND JUDGMENT

Another story in the Bible highlights our key concepts of mercy and forgiveness. Read about a sinful woman who was motivated to action after receiving God's forgiveness, while a Pharisee (an expert in the law) could not move beyond his judgments into mercy.

**Consider Luke 7:36-50 (MSG)**

One of the Pharisees asked him [Jesus] over for a meal. He went to the Pharisee's house and sat down at the dinner table. Just then a woman of the village, the town harlot, having learned that Jesus was a guest in the home of the Pharisee, came with a bottle of very expensive perfume and stood at his feet, weeping, raining tears on his feet. Letting down her hair, she dried his feet, kissed them, and anointed them with the perfume. When the Pharisee who had invited him saw this, he said to himself, "If this man was the prophet I thought he was, he would have known what kind of woman this is who is falling all over him."

Jesus said to him, "Simon, I have something to tell you."

"Oh? Tell me."

"Two men were in debt to a banker. One owed five hundred silver pieces, the other fifty. Neither of them could pay up, and so the banker canceled both debts. Which of the two would be more grateful?"

Simon answered, "I suppose the one who was forgiven the most."

"That's right," said Jesus. Then turning to the woman, but speaking to Simon, he said, "Do you see this woman? I came to your home; you provided no water for my feet, but she rained tears on my feet and dried them with her hair. You gave me no greeting, but from the time I arrived she hasn't quit kissing my feet. You provided nothing for freshening up, but she has soothed my feet with perfume. Impressive, isn't it? She was forgiven many, many sins, and so she is very, very grateful. If the forgiveness is minimal, the gratitude is minimal."

Then he spoke to her: "I forgive your sins."

That set the dinner guests talking behind his back: "Who does he think he is, forgiving sins!"

He ignored them and said to the woman, "Your faith has saved you. Go in peace."

**Let's Talk**

Why do you think the woman went to Jesus?

What did Jesus see in this woman that Simon did not? Do you think Jesus may see things in you and others that you do not see?

Whom do you most identify with: Simon (the judgmental Pharisee) or the sinful woman grateful for forgiveness? In what ways?

What is your reaction to Jesus' words to the woman? To you?

**Make It Personal**

If you are ready to forgive those with whom you were angry (including yourself), tear up or burn your anger letters. As you do, declare that you no longer want to be chained to unforgiveness and you choose to begin the process of forgiving that person.

*If you are in a group, the facilitator will lead everyone in a modified version of this activity.*

Another way to grant forgiveness is to express forgiveness through writing, artwork, journaling, or some other creative activity. Use the sample format below to write letters that you will *never* send. These letters allow forgiveness to settle into your heart.

Dear _____,

I forgive you for _____

_____

_____

I release myself and you from bitterness and unforgiveness.

## FORGIVING OURSELVES

The Enemy will use the past to keep us in bondage to the lie that God could never forgive us. If we continue to feel condemnation after we have fully repented, we are listening to this lie of the Enemy. When we believe this lie, we do not forgive ourselves. Forgiving ourselves is recognizing and accepting the truth of our great debt and receiving the great depth of God's forgiveness, grace, and mercy for us.

> **The woman forgiven of many sins** in the story was very grateful. Consider writing a gratitude list. Include things, people, circumstances, and opportunities with which God has blessed you, including the gift of His forgiveness. Gratitude helps alleviate shame and fear and opens the heart for a deeper relationship with God. Review this gratitude list or write a new one any time you need a reminder of God's grace and forgiveness.

We may not *feel* forgiven, but God's forgiveness is based on who He is, not on our feelings. Our emotions change, but God's nature and character do not. His forgiveness will never change. We choose to believe Him and take Him at His word, as the woman in the story did. Then we choose to accept His forgiveness, which allows us to forgive ourselves.

God forgives and chooses to no longer remember our sins. He has placed them at the bottom of the ocean, along with a *No fishing* sign!

Where is the god who can compare with you—wiping the slate clean of guilt, turning a blind eye, a deaf ear, to the past sins of your purged and precious people? You don't nurse your anger and don't stay angry long, for mercy is your specialty. That's what you love most. And compassion is on its way to us. You'll stamp out our wrongdoing. You'll sink our sins to the bottom of the ocean.

—Micah 7:18–19 (MSG)

God's forgiveness can release us from the ball and chain of our own unforgiveness. Holding on to sin after God has granted the freedom of forgiveness is like telling Him your sin is too great to be covered by the price He paid in sacrificing His Son.

I have swept away your sins like a cloud. I have scattered your offenses like the morning mist. Oh, return to me, for I have paid the price to set you free.

—Isaiah 44:22 (NCV)

## OUR LOSSES

Forgiving ourselves includes giving ourselves permission to grieve the losses resulting from our choices and to release them to God. Moving out of denial and processing emotional blocks brings us to the place where we can accept God's gift of grief. Grief is the normal process that helps us deal with the inevitable losses we all experience in our lives. As you name the things abortion has taken away, you can release these to God. Though this is not an easy process, God promises comfort and mercy.

The LORD wants to show his mercy to you. He wants to rise and comfort you.

—Isaiah 30:18 (NCV)

**Spend some quiet time with the Lord.** Begin to contemplate some of your losses, which include your child. Author Pat Layton suggests that you consider "those things—opportunities, people, relationships, experiences or feelings—that abortion either has taken away from you or never allowed you to experience."[15] Journal about these things.

You may wish to paraphrase the prophet Jeremiah's prayer (8:18) as you write about your losses: "God, You are my comfort when I am very sad and when I am afraid."

An important step in being able to fully grieve our loss of a child and experience closure is naming our child. This unique identity we give our child gives us a focus for our previously unexpressed grief so we may release deeper emotions. A name also dignifies our child and validates his or her value. This may be a difficult step, but it will bring you to a place of deeper healing.

**Make It Personal**

Reflect back on Psalm 139 from chapter 2 (see page 47). God knows you, and He knows your child. Spend some quiet time in prayer and ask the Lord to help you begin to understand who your child was (for example, gender, features, and so on). This may take time or several prayer sessions. Prayerfully consider a name for your child and write it down, along with any other description you may receive from the Lord. This will help you begin to fully and appropriately grieve your loss.

Psalm 139 also states that God is always with you and will bless you as you grieve:

> You go before me and follow me. You place your hand of blessing on my head.
>
> —Psalm 139:5

You have received God's gift of grace and have begun the process of forgiving others. The next chapter focuses on releasing your guilt and sorrow as you allow yourself to grieve the loss of your child(ren). Continue to persevere on this path—you are almost there!

### Journey Further

Read Psalm 61, a prayer for deliverance from others who have hurt you. Also read Psalm 138, a prayer for renewal.

# FELICIA

*A Story of Forgiving Others*

The chapter on forgiving others and ourselves was profoundly life changing for me. It unearthed dormant emotions and beliefs about forgiveness in my life. I didn't realize how wounded I was by others' words and deeds toward me. I was walking around with multiple festering wounds with unclean Band-Aids. This chapter helped me examine and address these old wounds with a new perspective.

When I was reminded of the wounds, all the emotions would flood back to me as if I were reliving the ordeal, and I would replay the situation over and over in my mind. I had yet to let go and truly forgive, and I was holding people hostage for the things they had said or done.

In some cases I didn't forgive myself for the role I had played.

In the section "Fundamentals of Forgiveness" I learned that forgiving those people didn't mean we would have the same relationship as before the wound occurred. I could pray for them and forgive them, and forgive myself for my part, but I did not have to let them back into my life to repeat the wound.

I also learned that it is not beneficial to attack them and make them accountable for their role in the argument. I realized that some people are just not going to take ownership for their part, and that is not what real forgiveness looks like. It is okay to let go of some relationships and people for God to make room for others who are supposed to be in your life. It is important to learn to develop healthy boundaries, learn how to forgive, and remember to forgive yourself.

Forgiveness is key to my relationship with God. If I cannot forgive, God is not going to forgive me no matter how wrong the other person is. God is just and righteous. His thoughts are higher than my thoughts, but most of all, He is the judge, not me.

Throughout this lesson God brought many applications of forgiveness to show me how important it is to Him for me to grasp and put into practice. He was really working on my heart and showing me in the process the importance of forgiveness: that if I release the person who hurt me, accept the things I cannot change, and give the emotions attached to that hurt to God, I am practicing forgiveness.

# ANNETTE

*A Story of Forgiving Myself*

I came to realize that God had forgiven me and it was time I forgave myself. I did not need to carry the burden of this any longer. I began to pray and asked God to help me forgive myself. It was difficult at first, because I really didn't want to forgive myself, but once I said the words God took it from there, and the prayers came easily after that.

I slowly started to forgive myself and, as I did, I was able to open my heart and accept the fact that I had lost a child. I did not want to acknowledge that I became a mother the moment a life was created inside of me. This was a hard fact for me to swallow.

This fact caused my heart great pain but at the same time I was relieved to feel this pain. Because now that I could feel it, I could process and release the emotions that came with it. For over a decade, I had suppressed this pain, but that didn't make it go away. It was always there hiding beneath the surface, and my body was working overtime trying to manage this pain in other ways.

Forgiveness was essential to my healing and peace of mind. Once I was able to forgive myself, I was able to recognize and begin to grieve the loss of my child.

Looking back, I am overwhelmed by God's grace in my life and how He has made so much good come from so many of my mistakes. No matter what difficulties you are facing, there is nothing that can't be overcome with God by your side. His love for you is overflowing, and He will never leave you. He is always with you, patiently waiting for you to seek His help, so He can fill your heart with joy and give you peace.

CHAPTER 7

# ALLOW TIME TO GRIEVE

*"He will wipe every tear from their eyes.*
*There will be no more death" or mourning or crying or pain,*
*for the old order of things has passed away.*
—REVELATION 21:4 (NIV)

*They are blessed who grieve, for God will comfort them.*
—MATTHEW 5:4 (NCV)

Grief is a natural, healthy response to the losses brought by abortion. As noted in the previous chapter, grief is a gift from God to help us release the pain of loss. Until you acknowledge and grieve the loss of your child, you simply manage the pain of unresolved grief and sorrow.

The tangle of emotions you have felt and the steps you've taken thus far are all a part of the grieving process. You have made tremendous progress, although it is not yet over. In this short chapter, may you see the rays of hope as you spend time honoring your lost child.

## HEALTHY TEARS

Grieving is a process unique to each individual, and it may take time. It is healthy to release tears brought about by the losses identified in the previous chapter. Some women may be afraid to cry for fear they will drown in painful emotion. They may fear losing control or that the pain will get worse. But we cannot heal if we don't feel. Hear God's promise to be with you through the deep waters of grief:

### Consider Isaiah 43:1–3

Do not be afraid, for I have ransomed you. I have called you by name; you are mine. When you go through deep waters, I will be with you. When you go through rivers of difficulty, you will not drown. When you walk through the fire of oppression, you will not be burned up; the flames will not consume you. For I am the LORD, your God, the Holy One of Israel, your Savior.

## WHERE IS THE BABY?

Once we've accepted that one of our losses was our children, we may question what happened to our babies. In chapter 2, we began to see that God knows us before we are formed (Jeremiah 1:5). Each of us has a unique, personal, eternal soul from the moment of conception, including our children. Our children did not experience a life of sin that may have kept them from heaven. Thus, our children's blameless souls entered into the presence of the Lord as spiritual, eternal beings.[16]

### Consider 1 Corinthians 15:42–44

It is the same way with the resurrection of the dead. Our earthly bodies are planted in the ground when we die, but they will be raised to live forever. Our bodies are buried in brokenness, but they will be raised in glory. They are buried in weakness, but they will be raised in strength. They are buried as natural human bodies, but they will be raised as spiritual bodies. For just as there are natural bodies, there are also spiritual bodies.

### Let's Talk

What hope does this verse give you regarding your child?

Think back to the story of Nathan confronting David for his sin over Bathsheba, in chapter 1 (on page 24). Read this story again (2 Samuel 12:1–13) as a reminder. The rest of the story is that David's sin was the reason his son did not survive. This is similar to the situation of those who have aborted their children. Yet David had hope that he would one day see his son again.[17]

### Consider 2 Samuel 12:13–23 (NIV)

Nathan replied, "The LORD has taken away your sin. You are not going to die. But because by doing this you have shown utter contempt for the LORD, the son born to you will die."

After Nathan had gone home, the LORD struck the child that Uriah's wife had borne to David, and he became ill. David pleaded with God for the child. He fasted and spent the nights lying in sackcloth on the ground. The elders of his household stood beside him to get him up from the ground, but he refused, and he would not eat any food with them.

On the seventh day the child died. David's attendants were afraid to tell him that the child was dead, for they thought, "While the child was still living, he wouldn't listen to us when we spoke to him. How can we now tell him the child is dead? He may do something desperate."

David noticed that his attendants were whispering among themselves, and he realized the child was dead. "Is the child dead?" he asked.

"Yes," they replied, "he is dead."

Then David got up from the ground. After he had washed, put on lotions and changed his clothes, he went into the house of the LORD and worshiped. Then he went to his own house, and at his request they served him food, and he ate.

His attendants asked him, "Why are you acting this way? While the child was alive, you fasted and wept, but now that the child is dead, you get up and eat!"

He answered, "While the child was still alive, I fasted and wept. I thought, 'Who knows? The LORD may be gracious to me and let the child live.' But now that he is dead, why should I go on fasting? Can I bring him back again? I will go to him, but he will not return to me."

**Let's Talk**

What reason did David give for ending his fast?

Where did David suggest that he would see his son? Do you believe you will go to your child one day? How do you imagine this reunion?

## MEMORIAL

The Bible contains other stories about grief and mourning. Joseph was a man who loved his father Jacob deeply, and grieved the loss of him when he died. As part of his mourning, he held a service to honor him:

> Joseph threw himself on his father and wept over him and kissed him.
> . . . When they arrived at the threshing floor of Atad, near the Jordan
> River, they held a very great and solemn memorial service, with a seven-
> day period of mourning for Joseph's father. The local residents, the
> Canaanites, watched them mourning at the threshing floor of Atad.
> Then they renamed that place (which is near the Jordan) Abel-mizraim,
> for they said, "This is a place of deep mourning for these Egyptians."
>
> —Genesis 50:1, 10–11

**Make It Personal**

Spend time alone with God to prepare your heart for a private service to remember your child, as Joseph did for his father. Honoring your child will help you transform your pain into hope. If you are in a group, this service will be shared together.

If you are reading this book on your own, invite your support person to join you for a personal memorial service. You may wish to include soft music to create a mood of peace. You or your support person may want to share a special Scripture or prayer. Consider lighting a candle for each child you are honoring as a symbol of his or her eternal soul.

Pray and ask the Lord to give you guidance as you write a letter or poem, or create art or a song to your child, sharing what your heart desires to express to your child. You may choose to read this aloud at your service and release your child to the Lord.

A sample prayer to close the service could be, *Thank You, Lord, that You promised to prepare a place for us so that we may be with You forever* (see John 14:2–3).

Afterward, you may wish to plant a flower or tree somewhere special, create a piece of art, or place something special in your home as an ongoing way to remember your child. Consider something that is meaningful to you as a way to honor the memory of your child.

*If you are in a group, the facilitator will lead everyone
in a modified version of this activity.*

## GOD'S HEART

As you mourn the loss of your child, remember that God promises to trade your sorrows for joy and turn your mourning into dancing. Hear God's heart to restore His people in the following verses:

> Then young women of Israel will be happy and dance, the young men and old men also. I will change their sadness into happiness; I will give them comfort and joy instead of sadness.
>
> —Jeremiah 31:13 (NCV)

> LORD, remember my suffering and my misery, my sorrow and trouble. Please remember me and think about me. But I have hope when I think of this: The LORD's love never ends; his mercies never stop. They are new every morning; LORD, your loyalty is great. I say to myself, "The LORD is mine, so I hope in him."
>
> —Lamentations 3:19–24 (NCV)

> I will exalt you, LORD, for you rescued me. You refused to let my enemies triumph over me. O LORD my God, I cried to you for help, and you restored my health.
>
> You brought me up from the grave, O LORD. You kept me from falling into the pit of death.
>
> Sing to the LORD, all you godly ones! Praise his holy name. For his anger lasts only a moment, but his favor lasts a lifetime! Weeping may last through the night, but joy comes with the morning.
>
> —Psalm 30:1–5

Give yourself time to mourn and experience the range of emotions that come with it. Know that there will come a time for dancing in the future. The next chapter will consider the hope of the future.

May the Lord strengthen and comfort you as you allow yourself to grieve the loss of your child.

## JOURNEY FURTHER

Read Psalm 126 to remind you that your tears will reap a harvest of joy.

Ask the Lord to give you guidance as you create something or write to your child. Take the time to express all the things you want to say to your child but have never said. If you are in a group, bring this with you to your service.

# MONIQUE

*For My Son, Kaman*

I thought about you today. And I tried so hard to suppress those thoughts but they wouldn't go away. So I let them go on as I imagined what you would have been like. Soft, sweet, with beautiful brown eyes, and a curious mind—like me. My beautiful baby. Oh, how I long to see your face, to feel your touch, for us to embrace.

And I cried for you today. Because there's this longing in my heart that wishes you were here. But you're not here. And past all of my pain, hurt, guilt, and shame is the reality that I never even got to hold you. I cried for you today because I know you would have been great. A world changer with purpose, destined for success.

I dreamed about you today. And in that dream we were together again. Yes, we connected again. And we had a heart-to-heart. And I cried and told you how sorry I was and how much I really do love you. You wiped my eyes and told me everything would be okay, that I'd see you one day.

So I smiled for you today, because I know I shall see you again on that glorious day in heaven where our eternal lives together will begin. You and me forever. This time, our bond will never be broken.

My beautiful baby—I thought of you today.

# MELISSA

*A Story of Grieving*

I have been blessed with not having to attend too many funerals besides the memorial service our group held. But the feelings were the same as at a funeral. I dreaded it. I was anxious. My heart fluttered and my stomach did flips when I thought about it. That's when the finality of abortion really hit me. I worked harder and longer on the grief lesson than I did on any of the other lessons. And I realized that had we not held a memorial service, I would have done what I always do when it's too hard: Just stuff it; ignore it.

But that's no longer possible. I have to face my Goliaths. In every aspect of my life.

All the work that preceded this chapter was so worth it. Then we came to the part where we were able to honor our children. It was the biggest blessing for me, because it was a huge part of my healing.

Again, I'm not very good at facing the large problems in my life. I would put my head in the sand and hope the problem would go away and all would be okay. As I painfully know, that strategy never works. We have to face the things in life that are difficult.

The memorial service was difficult. Partially, it was because it was not the final destination on the road to discovery and recovery for me, but really it was just the beginning. This service was the one thing I could do for my children here on earth, and I wanted my part to be perfect for them.

Thanks to my abortion recovery group and the ladies who stood beside me (and I beside them), this was possible. I will be forever grateful.

# CHAPTER 8

# DARE TO HOPE

*Forget the former things; do not dwell on the past.*
*See, I am doing a new thing! Now it springs up; do you not perceive it?*
*I am making a way in the wilderness and streams in the wasteland.*
—ISAIAH 43:18–19 (NIV)

*You have turned my mourning into joyful dancing.*
*You have taken away my clothes of mourning and clothed me with joy,*
*that I might sing praises to you and not be silent.*
*O LORD my God, I will give you thanks forever!*
—PSALM 30:11–12

As you near the end of this path, you may sense a shift in your story as your season of mourning transforms into a new season of hope. Grieving is a process unique to everyone, and there is no set amount of time that you may spend in mourning. The good news is that God is with you. And His comfort, grace, and love infuse every season of your life.

> For everything there is a season, a time for every activity under heaven. . . .
> A time to cry and a time to laugh. A time to grieve and a time to dance.
> —Ecclesiastes 3:1, 4

Sometimes emotions are triggered by certain events, dates, people, or other things. God is still with us when these moments happen; they are here only for a season, and a new season will come again. Sadness over your loss may remain, but how you view and experience the loss will change over time.

## OTHER CONCERNS

Along this path you may have become aware of issues (perhaps from the past), unresolved conflicts, relational struggles, or other concerns for which additional healing should be pursued. This may be through another abortion recovery group, a pastor, a counselor, or a support or recovery group for other issues. For example, sexual struggles and past sexual abuse are not uncommon among women who have had an abortion. Seeking additional help and support is strongly encouraged. Resources for this and various other concerns are listed on page 179.

The sexual intimacy that led to the unplanned pregnancy may have created an unhealthy soul bond between you and your partner. These bonds can lead to a distorted image of relationships, intimacy, and yourself. Breaking these bonds can bring deeper healing and a healthier view of relationships and the self. The supplemental materials section includes information on breaking unhealthy sexual soul bonds (see page 171). This important exercise might take time and, if you are in a group, may be offered as an additional session.

**Make It Personal**
Using the timeline you began in chapter 5, consider whether any other issues may need to be addressed in your life, such as unresolved conflicts, difficulties, or traumas. Ask God for guidance on whether you should pursue further healing and in what way. Also note patterns in your life you may learn from in making future decisions.

### New Beginning
The memorial service brought tangible closure to one season or chapter in our lives, but the rest of the book is just beginning. Read the story of ten men with leprosy, a skin disease, who received healing and a new beginning from Jesus.

**Consider Luke 17:11–19**

As Jesus continued on toward Jerusalem, he reached the border between Galilee and Samaria. As he entered a village there, ten men with leprosy stood at a distance, crying out, "Jesus, Master, have mercy on us!"

He looked at them and said, "Go show yourselves to the priests." And as they went, they were cleansed of their leprosy.

One of them, when he saw that he was healed, came back to Jesus, shouting, "Praise God!" He fell to the ground at Jesus' feet, thanking him for what he had done. This man was a Samaritan.

Jesus asked, "Didn't I heal ten men? Where are the other nine? Has no one returned to give glory to God except this foreigner?" And Jesus said to the man, "Stand up and go. Your faith has healed you."

**Let's Talk**

The men asked Jesus for mercy. How has Jesus been merciful to you?

How did the ten men react when they were cleansed? How do you relate to these men? Are you more like the Samaritan, or the other nine?

How can you thank or give glory to God for His healing work?

When we believe in and accept Christ's healing work in our lives, we are made new in Him. Our life story has been renewed as we traveled this path.

**Consider Ephesians 2:4–6 (NCV)**

But God's mercy is great, and he loved us very much. Though we were spiritually dead because of the things we did against God, he gave us new life with Christ. You have been saved by God's grace.

**Let's Talk**

In what ways have you been given a "new life" on this journey? By whose work and why?

**Consider Colossians 3:1–4 (MSG)**

So if you're serious about living this new resurrection life with Christ, *act* like it. Pursue the things over which Christ presides. Don't shuffle along, eyes to the ground, absorbed with the things right in front of you. Look up, and be alert to what is going on around Christ—that's where the action is. See things from *His* perspective. Your old life is dead. Your new life, which is your *real* life—even though invisible to spectators—is with Christ in God. *He* is your life.

**Let's Talk**

How can a focus on Christ's perspective help you pursue a new life? Keep in mind that having a new life does not mean we are free from struggles, but that we are transformed by them. Consider again your timeline and any patterns of God's hand in your story thus far.

According to Pastor Scott Johnson of Oakbrook Church, we may drift away from this new life story under any of the following circumstances:[18]

- We do not fully accept Jesus and do not communicate with Him regularly through prayer and His Word, the Bible.
- We go back to our old identity, following old patterns and old ways of thinking, believing, and behaving, and caring more about how people see us than how God sees us.
- We fail to follow Jesus' teachings and ways in our everyday lives.
- We let go of the memory of what God has done for us: His forgiveness, healing, and love for us.

## RENEWING MINDS

To put this new life story into practice, it's important to continually allow the Holy Spirit to renew our hearts and minds, which will help us change our old behavior patterns.

### Consider Ephesians 4:21–24

Since you have heard about Jesus and have learned the truth that comes from him, throw off your old sinful nature and your former way of life, which is corrupted by lust and deception. Instead, let the Spirit renew your thoughts and attitudes. Put on your new nature, created to be like God—truly righteous and holy.

### Let's Talk

What are some ways you can prepare to guard your mind against the Enemy? Think of the powerful weapons you read about in chapter 2.

Consider your Stronghold of Truth wall from chapter 4. What other resources has God given you to renew your mind?

We cooperate with the Holy Spirit in renewing our minds by refusing to believe the Enemy's lies about us and by not focusing on the old negative thoughts and attitudes we once had. It is important to have a plan and be ready when the Enemy attacks your mind and tries to make you remember the old lies you believed for so long.

One way to prepare yourself is to maintain "an attitude of gratitude" for God's provisions. Remember what God has done in your life so far, and stay connected to Him. Continue to draw closer to God and develop a deep relationship with Him, listening for His heart to speak to yours.

### Consider Colossians 1:21–23 (MSG)

You yourselves are a case study of what he does. At one time you all had your backs turned to God, thinking rebellious thoughts of him, giving him trouble every chance you got. But now, by giving himself completely at the Cross, actually *dying* for you, Christ brought you over to God's side and put your lives together, whole and holy in his presence. You don't walk away from a gift like that! You stay grounded and steady in that bond of trust, constantly tuned in to the Message, careful not to be distracted or diverted. There is no other Message—just this one. Every creature under heaven gets this same Message.

### Let's Talk

How can you stay grounded in a bond of trust with Christ?

## SUMMARY OF THE PRINCIPLES

To live this new life, it is also important to apply the lessons of this journey to other areas of life. Here is a summary of the principles from this path:

1. In the first chapter, we learned to acknowledge how our choices affect our lives and that when we share our story with God and others, secrets begin to lose their power over us. We also realized that we are powerless to heal or restore ourselves, but the light of truth gives us hope. We discovered that God desires to transform our story.

2. Next, we learned the importance of facing the truth about actions in our lives, rather than denying them, hiding them, or blaming others.

We learned more about ourselves, our choices, and about God. We also received an action plan to counter the Enemy so we could choose to accept the invitation to continue the journey to wholeness.

3. We then began to inventory the emotions and behaviors that filled our lives as a result of our choices. First, we reviewed various types of anger and explored our own anger. Then we had an opportunity to express our anger in a healthy way. We received a spiritual tool that will help us to process anger in healthy ways in the future.

4. We then looked at depression, guilt, and shame. We learned that guilt can lead us to turn to God for transformation, while shame can become a stronghold over us. We released our shame as we tore down strongholds of the Enemy's lies and built a protective wall of God's truth, about His love for us and His view of us, in order to conquer shame.

5. Next we learned about God's free gift of grace and forgiveness. We considered barriers to accepting grace, and reviewed God's character and Jesus' sacrifice for us. We had the opportunity to humbly ask to be forgiven, and we received or created a tangible gift to remind us that our forgiveness was granted through Jesus.

6. Once forgiven by God, we discovered more elements of forgiveness so we can extend forgiveness to others. We considered the power of prayer as a tool to help us make the choice to forgive others. We learned that forgiving ourselves means accepting and receiving God's grace and allowing ourselves to grieve our losses.

7. Once we processed all the emotions and shared them with God, we were able to identify and grieve our losses tangibly. We connected with God in prayer to mourn our losses and receive His comfort. We learned that God promises to trade our sorrows for joy as we continue to journey with Him.

## Serving Others

These principles can be practiced in other areas of life on an ongoing basis. They can also be shared with others who may be struggling. The amazing thing is that the more we help others, the more we grow and learn.

**Consider 2 Corinthians 1:3–5**

All praise to God, the Father of our Lord Jesus Christ. God is our merciful Father and the source of all comfort. He comforts us in all our troubles so that we can comfort others. When they are troubled, we will be able to give them the same comfort God has given us. For the more we suffer for Christ, the more God will shower us with his comfort through Christ.

**Let's Talk**

The word "comfort" here also means "encourage." In what ways has God comforted or encouraged you through this healing path?

How might you be able to encourage others? Brainstorm some ideas with your group or support person.

Comforting others and giving glory to God may include sharing your story of healing. Before you choose to do this, consider your motives for sharing, what benefits may result, and whether any other participants from your experience may be harmed by your sharing. Also consider how you tell someone, seeking the right opportunity. Always seek guidance from the Lord before sharing your story with anyone privately or publicly.

Pray and ask God to guide you as to how you can help others by sharing what you've learned and gained through this study.

God has done a great work in you, and He will continue to work in you as He leads you. Your part is to cooperate with Him in this journey, allowing Him to do His work, and asking Him how you may participate in His grand, adventurous story.

> God began doing a good work in you, and I am sure he will continue it until it is finished when Jesus Christ comes again.
>
> —Philippians 1:6 (NCV)

**Make It Personal**

Create a personal plan of action to continue pursuing this transformed life story. Consider all the tools you've gained in this journey and how you can use them in other areas of your life. Answer the questions below to guide you as you begin thinking about your personal action plan. As you write your plan, consider the core elements we've shared—truth, prayer, and community.

1. What spiritual tools have I gained?
2. Is there anything I need to stop doing?
3. What actions or ways of thinking might I want to start?
4. What actions or ideas could be changed?
5. Who may be a safe person or community for me to share with?
6. What other areas in my life might I need to focus on now? How can I begin addressing them?

## JOURNEY FURTHER

Read Psalm 116, and lift it up as a prayer of gratitude to God for delivering you from trouble. Also read Psalm 16, a prayer of faith and trust.

If you are in a group, an additional session may be offered to break sexual soul bonds. If not, complete this powerful exercise on your own and invite your support person to conclude your time with prayer.

# GAYLE

*The Heart*

*The heart is deceitful above all things. . . .*
*Who can understand it?*
—JEREMIAH 17:9 (NIV)

I've followed my heart, instead of Your Spirit, many times, I must admit.
It led me to a barren place, lonely and far from You.
I knew I wouldn't last long there. I knew I couldn't continue.
I knew I had to do something. I couldn't stay in that place.
But what was I supposed to do? There were issues I couldn't face.
There were things I didn't want to give up . . . things I thought were best
    for me.
Things that I thought were very good, for the future I couldn't see.
But You, the jealous God that You are, showed me in various ways
That this wasn't the place for me. Your mercy wouldn't allow me to stay.
Well, I did have the choice to stay where I was, and not have any peace.
But if I wanted to live an abundant life, all self-reliance would have
    to cease.
So with much pain, I gave up those things that I'd thought were the best
    for me.
I decided to give You the throne of my heart . . . to let the Holy
    Spirit lead.
Since then, my life hasn't been problem-free, but You've shown Your
    faithfulness.
You've also shown Your sovereignty and blessed me with what You
    find best!

# MELISSA

## *The Rest of My Story*

I gave up to God and asked for His forgiveness. The Lord lovingly worked with me one-on-one, and His light was so healing. He did so much for me during that time while I researched and found a couple of groups of women who rallied around me and helped me. One was the Silent No More Awareness Campaign. One of the founders guided me to a local abortion healing group. Forty years after my abortion, I was finally ready to reveal my secret and start the healing process.

During that eight-week period, I realized what God had done for me and was continuing to do. The healing was almost immediate. I was so relieved to be in a safe place where I could talk about my abortion and my feelings to other women, who understood because they had experienced it as well.

When I realized abortion was a trauma, it was so freeing for me. I was then able to understand why I felt and acted the way I did.

Once the Light of Truth hits the secret, it can no longer grow. It shrinks and eventually goes away. Today, I am a different woman. I'm redeemed and forgiven, and I have forgiven myself. God exchanged a crown of beauty for ashes—festive praise instead of mourning.

Today, I am married to a wonderful, supportive, godly man who loves me in spite of myself! He is truly my rock, and I am so thankful God put him in my life.

Since I was never able to have children of my own, the Lord sent me all sorts of young people to fill my life and my home. My husband and I were blessed with a large house and many bedrooms that we subsequently filled with young missionaries, interns, visiting nationals, and a group of young international women we met at church. We had such fun with them and were able to speak into their lives and have a wonderful time together—usually centered around meals. Many of these relationships remain intact today.

I have been given the desire to speak into other women's lives. Through a local women's clinic, I have been given the awesome responsibility and opportunity of walking alongside and working with women who have been through the pain and trauma of abortion. I was given the opportunity to share my testimony with my church and record a radio segment on a

Christian radio station. I am also the regional coordinator of the Silent No More Awareness Campaign for Idaho.

Once the silence is broken, it is so freeing! God is a God of second chances, and He is so gracious and faithful. Without His Holy Spirit working in and through me, today I wouldn't be here. Healing is possible and is there for the asking. In John 14:27, Jesus tells us, "I am leaving you with a gift—peace of mind and heart. And the peace I give is a gift the world cannot give. So don't be troubled or afraid."

That gift is there for the asking.

# JAMIE

### *The Rest of My Story*

When I surrendered to God, He spoke straight to my heart at every church service I attended, in every song I sang, and in every quiet moment I shared with Him. He calmed me and whispered, "It will be okay" and "I've got you" and "You are Mine."

It didn't happen all at once, but from the moment I looked up from the bottom of the pit I was in, He answered. He had been trying all along to get my attention. I believed in Him and prayed on occasion, but I didn't want Him to get in the way of what I wanted to do.

God pulled me out of the pit. He began a restoration process in my heart. He began healing my painful wounds. He put a passion in my soul for women who have experienced the things I experienced because of an unplanned pregnancy. That passion led me to volunteer at a pregnancy center so I could share my story and help others see that abortion is not the easy or quick answer they are looking for.

The center required volunteers to go through a healing Bible study if they had an abortion in their past. I didn't think I needed it, but God used that study to further the healing He had already started. I saw how my abortion was connected to so many other issues. I was able to forgive all those involved in my abortion decision and let go of anger and resentment, and I began to forgive myself for what I had done.

A few years later, God led me through another journey of healing in another state. This time I was able to recognize and honor the child I lost. Entrusting her to Jesus healed a piece of my heart I hadn't known was still broken.

God is still restoring and healing my soul, and He will continue to do so until I see Him face to face. But He has brought me a *long* way from lying face down in the dark pit I couldn't get out of.

I am very happily married to a loving, godly man. We were dating when God began His work in me. He was one of the first people I "came out" to about my abortion. He is my biggest supporter and has encouraged me to share my story with others. We have two beautiful children whom we love more than we could have imagined. I tell them about their sister who is waiting for them in heaven.

I am not haunted by my mistakes now, the way I was years ago. I will always regret and confess my sin of aborting my child, but Jesus' blood has washed me clean. There are consequences and deep hurts I still feel because of my selfish decision. But I desire for God's light to shine through the darkness of my story to reach others.

Today, I want to reach those who are experiencing a crisis pregnancy and those who made the wrong decision, as I did, because there is still hope. I now volunteer with a pregnancy resource center and have the opportunity to share my story and help other women find healing and hope after the pain of an abortion.

In Jesus Christ, there is hope for all.

# A STORY TRANSFORMED

*Our faces, then, are not covered. We all show*
*the Lord's glory, and we are being changed to be like him.*
*This change in us brings ever greater glory,*
*which comes from the Lord, who is the Spirit.*
—2 CORINTHIANS 3:18 (NCV)

As you close out this guidebook, take time to reflect on how far you've come. You have persevered in a remarkable journey on this path to recovery. You were courageous and brought your story out of hiding and allowed the light of God to penetrate the darkness. As you traveled into that light, God began healing and changing you.

We met another woman along this path who was changed by Jesus as well. Do you recognize the Samaritan woman from our introduction in the story below?

> Then Jesus told her, "I AM the Messiah!"
> . . . The woman left her water jar beside the well and ran back to the village, telling everyone, "Come and see a man who told me everything I ever did! Could he possibly be the Messiah?" So the people came streaming from the village to see him.
> —John 4:26, 28-30

The woman who once avoided the people of the village—perhaps out of fear, bitterness, and shame—now ran to the people, eager to share her new discovery of Jesus, the Messiah. He exposed her thirst for love and offered her the living water of life and love that can never run dry, no matter what the past hides. The woman's encounter with Jesus transformed her from evader to emissary. When you began this healing path, Jesus offered you that living water, and your experiences with Him have also been transforming you with each step. Perhaps, like this woman, you may choose to encourage others to "come and see" the offer He makes.

This book started with Laurie's metaphor encouraging you to examine the "flower weeds" that were crowding your life story. It seems fitting to end by returning to this metaphor. As you trudged this path, you have diligently inspected and uprooted weeds of lies, anger, guilt, and shame. You have acknowledged and named the losses that enabled the choking weeds to enter. You may continue to grieve these losses for some time. But as you nurture the seeds of truth, forgiveness, mercy, and grace that were sown along the way, the grief will soften and you will grow stronger. In due season, you will begin to harvest tasty "vegetables" like relationships, opportunity, hope, peace, and even joy.

As in all gardens, other weeds may spring up in your life occasionally, and you will need to examine and pull them. But God, our gardener, has planted healing and redemption in your story. He has planted seeds for you to cultivate with Him continually. He desires for you to follow His lead as He designs a healthy, beautiful garden in your life story.

> In simple humility, let our gardener, God, landscape you with the Word, making a salvation-garden of your life.
>
> —James 1:21 (MSG)

With God's help, you have uncovered, discovered, and recovered elements of your greater life story. Take some time to ponder some of the most meaningful steps of this journey and consider how He has transformed and is transforming your story. The exciting news is that He has more for you as you seek His light.

May the peace that comes from Christ dwell in your heart, and may God keep you and bless you as you continue your journey with Him. As we complete this path, I leave you this prayer of Jesus' follower Paul:

> I pray that the God who gives hope will fill you with much joy and peace while you trust in him. Then your hope will overflow by the power of the Holy Spirit.
>
> —Romans 15:13 (NCV)

# Supplemental Materials

# SAMPLE GROUP COMMITMENT FORM

*from page 1*

**MY STORY:** I began my abortion recovery journey with just one companion. We supported each other as we worked through the healing steps together using a post-abortion healing Bible study. This was a helpful start, but I didn't understand much about the Bible at the time, so in some areas I misunderstood the verses I read or could not relate them to my own story. Later I found that a group was more beneficial for me as we related to Bible stories, not just verses, and shared our experiences. Having "ground rules" or guidelines helped to keep us on track and to keep us focused on our own healing journey, while respecting and supporting each other.

---

Making a group commitment is a common practice among recovery or support groups. There are important core values that we must commit to as individuals and agree upon as a group to prepare and cultivate our healing path together.

**Priority.** The group meetings are a priority while we are in this group. Committed attendance is important for healing and for developing trust and comfort with sharing.

- I agree to contact the facilitators if an emergency arises and I am unable to attend the group session.
- If a session must be missed, I will meet with a facilitator before the next session.
- There is freedom to exit the group at any time during a session; however, we are also responsible to the group and I will explain why I chose to leave.

**Confidentiality.** Anything said in our group meetings and member-to-member is never repeated outside the meeting. This is a closed group, so what is shared here stays here. Guarding anonymity and confidentiality helps us build a safe environment.

**Preparation.** Reading the chapter and working through the material are important for recovery and healing, so we commit to completing assignments each week. The healing gained is influenced by the time and effort we put into the journey. Not completing chapters as we go along may hinder progress.

**Participation.** Each member has her own personal journey as well as a responsibility to the group and its members. We agree to participate in the group by honestly sharing our own thoughts, insights, feelings, and experiences briefly.

**Respect.** Everyone is unique, with a unique story, and we will not judge or criticize others as they share. We will respect the thoughts of others. We will show courtesy and listen to others and not interrupt them or try to "fix" or rescue them as they share. We will ask permission to offer feedback in a loving and supportive way to another member in the group and will respect her choice. Unsolicited advice is not permitted.

**Responsibility.** We are responsible for our own recovery and will be honest with ourselves and others. We will contact a facilitator or our support person if we are depressed and will not consider suicide or use destructive behaviors to "numb out."

**Accountability.** We are each accountable to the group as a whole. We will not come to the group session under the influence of nonprescription drugs or alcohol, so as to not disrupt the group.

**Expectations of facilitators.** This is a biblical healing group, not professional therapy. Facilitators are not licensed therapists; they are trained volunteers who wish to support and encourage others and share their own experience, strength, and hope.

_____    _____

I commit to all of the above (signature)                Date

# FURTHER QUESTIONS TO CONSIDER

*from page 27*

**MY STORY:** The first time I shared my abortion story with someone, I could remember very little. Perhaps this was because my mind distorted the memories to protect me from emotional pain, as often happens with a traumatic experience. Or perhaps it was simply because it had been so long since it happened. Either way, it is helpful to remember our stories in order to heal. Or, as I once heard someone say, "we can't tame it until we name it." It's okay if you don't remember certain aspects: more will be revealed to you as you grow in your healing.

---

To find peace from our abortion stories, we must break out of our denial and remember. Abortion can be a traumatic experience, and when we have traumatic experiences, the mind sometimes distorts the details of the memories as a protective device. We often try to block out details that are inconvenient or painful. These questions may help you to remember your own experience so you can truthfully process what happened.

- What was your life like at the time of pregnancy?
- How old were you?
- What were your family relationships like then?
- In what way, if any, was God part of your life then?
- Describe your relationship with the person who got you pregnant.
- Who, if anyone, was with you when you had the abortion?
- If you went to an abortion facility, did you see a counselor? If so, what was discussed? Describe the atmosphere, the staff, and how you felt at the facility.
- What type of abortion did you have?
- What do you remember about the experience?
- Do you remember anything you were thinking or feeling at the time?
- If you were at a facility, what do you remember about the recovery room? If you were not at a facility, where were you?
- What did you think and feel physically and emotionally as you recovered?
- If you were not at home, what do you remember about the ride home?
- Did you talk to anyone about the abortion afterward? Who did you talk to and what was the conversation like?

# FETAL DEVELOPMENT

*from page 47*

**MY STORY:** Through various twelve-step recovery programs, I learned that being "rigorously honest" with myself and another person was crucial in order to make progress on the path to transformation. For me, a difficult but important part of that honesty was owning up to my reasons for abortion and facing the reality of human development and the concept of "personhood."

---

The following timeline highlights key stages in a baby's development, from conception to birth. Science of human development affirms that we are "wonderfully complex" (Psalm 139:14)!

Note: While pregnancy is tracked from the date of the last menstrual period, this timeline follows fetal age, which begins at conception.

**Day 1:** Once fertilization occurs, the baby's chromosomes are all present, including those that determine gender. The embryo moves through the fallopian tube toward the uterus, where it attaches within the first week.

**Week 3:** The baby's nervous system begins forming, including what will become the brain.

**Week 6:** The heart beats. The baby has a separate blood supply and may have a different blood type than the mother does.

**Week 7:** Spontaneous movements, such as twitching of the trunk and limbs, occur.

**Week 8:** Fingers and facial features have formed. Bones start to grow. Digestive and sensory organs develop.

**Week 10:** Teeth and fingernails develop. Joints are in place, and the baby can make fists and flex limbs.

**Week 12:** All organs are present. A complete nervous system is in place and pain can be felt. This is the end of the first trimester. The baby is approximately four inches long and weighs about an ounce.

**Months 4–5:** Movement may be felt by the mother. Fingerprints form. Gender can be determined in an ultrasound. The baby can swallow and suck his or her thumb.

**Month 6:** The baby breathes amniotic fluid. Babies born prematurely at this stage may survive with medical care. This is the end of the second trimester. At one foot long, the baby weighs about two pounds.

**Months 7–8:** Hearing is fully developed, and the baby responds to external stimuli. Lungs are not yet mature.

**Month 9:** A baby born after 38 weeks is considered full term, though the third trimester officially ends at 40 weeks. Lungs are mature, and the baby is around 18–21 inches long and may weigh 7–10 pounds. The baby moves into a head-down position, ready for delivery.

For additional details and images of fetal development through the various stages of pregnancy, see books such as Peter Tallack's *In the Womb* (National Geographic, 2006) and Alexander Tsiaras's *From Conception to Birth* (Doubleday, 2002) or websites such as Just the Facts (www.justthefacts.org) or the Endowment for Human Development (www.ehd.org).

# RESPONSIBILITY AND INFLUENCE PIE 1

*from page 54*

**MY STORY:** I was a "blamer" from the start of my abortion story. I could not move forward until I began to look at whom, what, and why I blamed, because it kept me trapped in anger at other people, especially the boyfriend. We are all unique, so it is important for you to consider your own influences so you can move forward.

---

Think about the people or institutions involved in your abortion experience that you believe influenced you or share the responsibility for the abortion decision. Divide the pie below into pieces that reflect what you believe to be the percentage of each person or organization's involvement. (Examples include yourself; the father of your baby; your mother, father, or friends; the abortion clinic staff; the church.) There are no right or wrong answers; this is to help you understand where you are on the healing path.

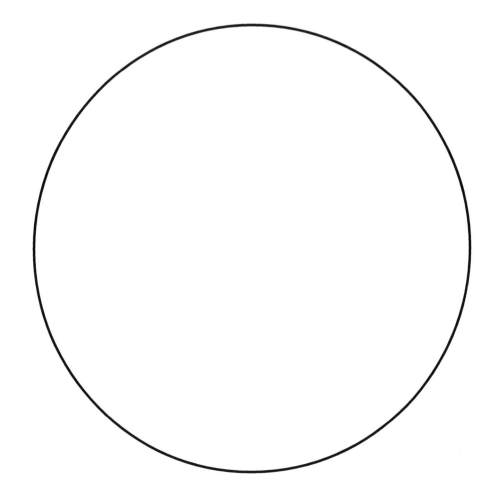

# Cool the Heat*

*from page 65*

**MY STORY:** My anger was a boiling pool of intense lava when I started my healing journey! My blaming and churning would smolder and eventually erupt sideways. I justified my anger and behavior until I began to learn biblical ways of examining, managing, and expressing my anger. I am grateful for my sponsor in my twelve-step program and for other resources from which I learned this! I am also grateful that in the order of the original twelve steps of recovery, forgiveness comes later, so I had time to process my anger. When it was time to forgive, my sponsor and other resources helped me through.

---

Review the following verses and consider how they relate to the way you cope with your anger. You may want to keep helpful steps and verses in a visible place as an anger-management guide.

**1. Search your heart and assess your primary emotion.** Does your anger come from insecurity, loss of control, guilt, unmet expectations, fear, pride, etc.? Or does it stem from an unjust wrong? Acknowledge your true emotions so you can respond properly.

> In your anger do not sin; when you are on your beds, search your hearts and be silent. —Psalm 4:4 (NIV 84)

**2. Control your immediate response.** Breathe deeply and ask God to help you manage the intensity of your anger. Take a time-out if needed to review your reaction.

> Understand this, my dear brothers and sisters: You must all be quick to listen, slow to speak, and slow to get angry. —James 1:19

---

\* These biblical ways of dealing with anger have been adapted from twelve-step recovery programs as well as from Charles Stanley's *Surviving in an Angry World: Finding Your Way to Personal Peace* (New York: Howard Books, 2010), 81, 85–86; Gary Chapman's *The Other Side of Love: Handling Anger in a Godly Way* (Chicago: Moody, 1999), 49, 72, 100; Pat Layton's *Surrendering the Secret: Healing the Heartbreak of Abortion* (Nashville, TN: LifeWay, 2008), 63; and Beth Moore's *Praying God's Word: Breaking Free from Spiritual Strongholds* (Nashville, TN: Broadman & Holman, 2000), 233, 235—all of which are excellent books to carry your healing further.

**3. Determine next steps.** Communicate honestly with others if you need to deal with an issue. Ask questions to clarify the situation, rather than assuming you know others' thoughts and intentions. Consider your own part in order to resolve issues with love.

> Why do you see the speck in your neighbor's eye, but do not notice the log in your own eye? Or how can you say to your neighbor, "Let me take the speck out of your eye," while the log is in your own eye? You hypocrite, first take the log out of your own eye, and then you will see clearly to take the speck out of your neighbor's eye.
> —Matthew 7:3–5 (NRSV)

> I urge Euodia and Syntyche to iron out their differences and make up. God doesn't want his children holding grudges. —Philippians 4:2 (MSG)

> And "don't sin by letting anger control you." Don't let the sun go down while you are still angry. —Ephesians 4:26

**4. Stop rehearsing old hurts, which can smolder into resentment and bitterness.** Instead, let go of anger and resentment and trust God to take care of your concerns and bring justice in His timing and in His way. Redirect your energy in a productive way to help others and choose forgiveness.

> Get rid of all bitterness, rage, anger, harsh words, and slander, as well as all types of evil behavior. Instead, be kind to each other, tenderhearted, forgiving one another, just as God through Christ has forgiven you.
> —Ephesians 4:31–32

> Make allowance for each other's faults, and forgive anyone who offends you. Remember, the Lord forgave you, so you must forgive others.
> —Colossians 3:13

**5. Slow down and share your anger honestly with God, perhaps with a letter or lamenting prayer.** Talk to Him about your fears and triggers. Confess it to others if appropriate. Express your anger in a safe manner.

> I call on the Lord in my distress, and he answers me. —Psalm 120:1 (NIV)

> Make this your common practice: Confess your sins to each other and pray for each other so that you can live together whole and healed.
> —James 5:16 (MSG)

# Responsibility and Influence Pie 2

## *from page 66*

**MY STORY:** Once I began to grasp my anger's purpose and learned to express my anger in a healthier way, my "blaming" began to shift. I began to consider my part more and to hold myself increasingly responsible.

---

After doing the work of chapter 3, your understanding of the influences involved in your abortion may have changed. Consider who you believe influenced or shares responsibility for the abortion decision. Divide the pie below into pieces that reflect what you now believe to be the percentage of each person or organization's involvement. (Examples include yourself; the father of your baby; your mother, father, or friends; the abortion clinic staff; and the church.) There are no right or wrong answers; this is to help you understand where you are on the healing path.

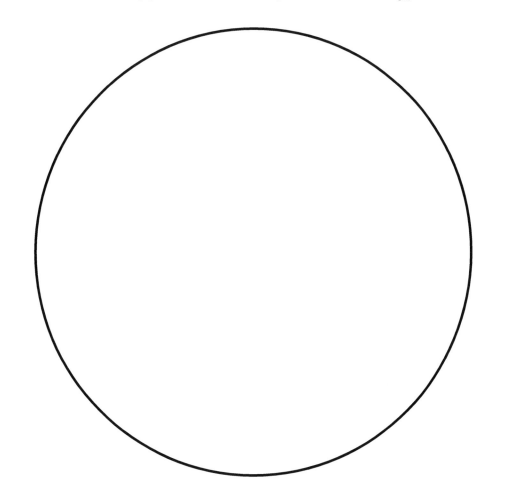

# Symptoms of Depression

*from page 71*

**MY STORY:** I coped with my abortion by repressing the memories and disassociating from it, so I did not struggle with depression. However, I've met women who do battle with depression following an abortion, to varying degrees.

---

Not everyone who is depressed experiences every symptom listed below. A person may experience only a few symptoms or may struggle with many of them. The severity of symptoms also varies among individuals. Women who have had an abortion tend to struggle most around anniversary dates (day of the abortion, day child was due, or holidays).

- Difficulty concentrating, remembering details, and making decisions
- Fatigue and decreased energy; feeling "slowed down"
- Feelings of guilt, worthlessness, and/or helplessness
- Feelings of hopelessness and pessimism nearly every day for at least two weeks
- Difficulty sleeping, early-morning wakefulness, or excessive sleeping
- Irritability, restlessness
- Loss of interest or pleasure in activities or hobbies once enjoyed
- Appetite and/or weight changes
- Persistent aches or pains, headaches, cramps, or digestive problems that do not ease even with treatment
- Persistent sad, anxious, or empty feelings
- Thoughts of suicide; suicide attempts

For other mental-health checklists, see https://www.webmd.com/first-aid/suicidal-thoughts-treatment and https://afsp.org/about-suicide/risk-factors-and-warning-signs/.

**If the above signs and symptoms describe you and are negatively affecting your life and relationships, please seek professional help.** The resource lists on page 179 give some options, or you can contact your local community's mental-health agency to direct you to further assistance.

# Strongholds Worksheets

### *from page 81*

**MY STORY:** I've heard it said that "where there is blame, there is shame." This was certainly the case for me, although I did not realize it until I was in recovery. Once the lava of anger started to cool, I felt the shame that plagued me for so many years after my abortion. I started to see the messages that I was nailing into my mind, heart, and soul, covering the concept of my identity. It was a relief to come across a list of "Truth Scriptures" from a cast-aside women's newsletter around that time. I can no longer find that original newsletter, but the truths I gained there have been echoed in various other Bible studies and online lists. The list in chapter 4 is a compilation of these.

---

The two illustrations on the following pages may be used instead of a group activity. If you are reading this book on your own, complete the walls and share them with your support person.

On the first stronghold illustration, the Stronghold of Lies, write within the blocks of the wall the shame-filled lies that you have heard or thought about yourself. Once complete, remove the page from the book and rip it into pieces, stating out loud your rejection of these lies. For example, if you wrote "I am a failure," say "I am *not* a failure."

On the second stronghold illustration, the Stronghold of Truth, write the truth you now know about yourself before God within the blocks of the wall. Once complete, remove the page from the book and post it somewhere where you will see it often, as a reminder and source of encouragement.

# Stronghold of Lies

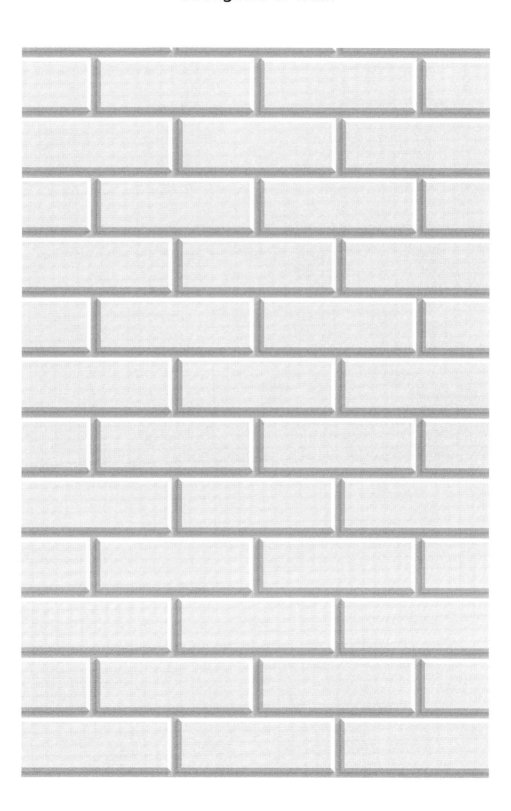

CUT HERE

# RESPONSIBILITY AND INFLUENCE PIE 3

*from page 82*

**MY STORY:** As I began to notice and reject the lies about myself and my identity, my view of "responsibility" and "influence" shifted again. I have learned that, in some way, we are all affected by circumstances, people (including family), or things, and we are accountable for the way we choose to respond to these influences. There is both influence and responsibility in our choices.

---

As you have dug deeper into your story and emotions, you may have gained another perspective on the influences on your abortion experience. Divide the pie below to depict your greater understanding that no one person or group bears total and complete responsibility.

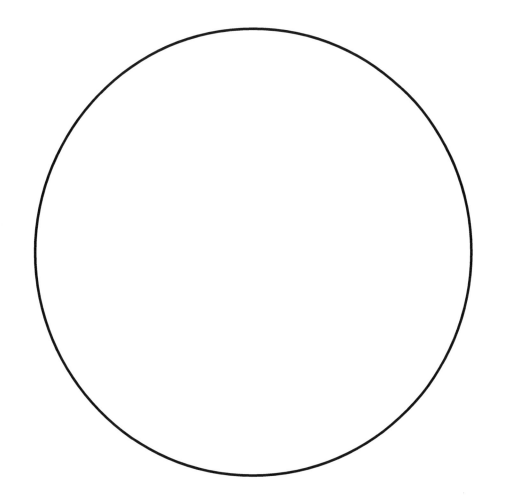

.

# Timeline Worksheet

*from pages 95 and 126*

**MY STORY:** I learned about the concept of a timeline before I even entered abortion recovery. It is a common exercise in the counseling and self-help fields, for a variety of purposes. In my case, creating a timeline helped me see themes or patterns in how I responded to circumstances and how I viewed God's hand in my life. This helped me to see additional areas in which I desired personal change and growth and to be grateful for God's grace.

---

As you look back at the various stages of your life, do you now see times when Jesus revealed Himself to you or was pursuing you? On the following chart, plot both positive and negative major life events, including spiritual ones. Identify the people and relationships that have been influential in your life, and note how and what you learned about God in each stage.

## My Timeline

- Plot positive and negative experiences, according to your personal scale of high/low.
- Plot major life events—relocations, deaths, births, traumatic events.
- Are there other issues to be addressed (such as unresolved conflict or trauma)?
- What areas have shaped who you are today, and how have you coped?
- What areas or patterns of God's movement do you see?
- What areas or patterns to learn from (coping mechanisms) do you see?

- - - - - - - CUT HERE - - - - - - -

**HIGH POINTS**

**AGE**

10   20   30   40   50   60

**LOW POINTS**

# WHO IS GOD?

*from page 97*

**MY STORY:** As I progressed in my healing and faith journey, I waivered at times in my beliefs about who God is and whether His grace really is for me. It seemed too good to be true! A friend gave me a list of characteristics of God to ponder, helping me relate to His ability and His desire to give grace.

---

Meditating on the character of God for 10–15 minutes a day can decrease anxiety and fear and open the heart to His grace.

God is . . .

**Love:** 1 John 4:8, " . . . for God is love"; Psalm 36:7, "How priceless is your unfailing love, O God!" (NIV).

**All-knowing:** 1 John 3:20, "For God is greater than our hearts, and he knows everything" (NRSV).

**Unchanging:** Malachi 3:6, "I the LORD do not change" (NCV).

**Our healer:** Psalm 147:3, "He heals the brokenhearted and binds up their wounds" (NIV); Psalm 107:19–20, "'LORD, help!' they cried in their trouble, and he saved them from their distress. He sent out his word and healed them, snatching them from the door of death."

**Patient:** 2 Peter 3:9, " . . . He is patient with you, not wanting anyone to perish, but everyone to come to repentance" (NIV).

**Just:** Numbers 14:18, "The LORD is slow to anger and filled with unfailing love, forgiving every kind of sin and rebellion. But he does not excuse the guilty"; Psalm 33:5, "The LORD loves righteousness and justice; the earth is full of his unfailing love" (NIV).

**Merciful, compassionate, faithful:** Psalm 86:15, "But you, O Lord, are a God of compassion and mercy, slow to get angry and filled with unfailing love and faithfulness"; Lamentations 3:21–23, "Yet this I call to mind and therefore I have hope: Because of the LORD's great love we are not consumed, for his compassions never fail. They are new every morning; great is your faithfulness" (NIV).

**Good:** Psalm 145:9, "The LORD is good to everyone. He showers compassion on all his creation."

**Our protector:** Psalm 18:2, "The LORD is my rock, my fortress and my deliverer; my God is my rock, in whom I take refuge, my shield and the horn of my salvation, my stronghold" (NIV).

**Powerful and sovereign:** Job 42:2, "I know that you [God] can do all things and that no plan of yours can be ruined" (NCV).

**Always present:** Hebrews 13:5, "Never will I leave you; never will I forsake you" (NIV).

# SEVERING SEXUAL SOUL BONDS*

*from page 126*

**MY STORY:** I struggled with promiscuity before and after my abortion. This behavior was a major contributor to my shame, insecurity, and confusion about emotional and physical intimacy—indeed, my fear of it. In my initial abortion recovery journey, I learned that the messages and lies I believed about myself and God influenced my abortion choice. Many of those lies were also tangled up with past promiscuous behavior.

Shortly after my journey into healing from my abortion, I attended a conference where I heard author Barbara Wilson speak about "sexual soul bonds." In order to renew my thoughts and attitudes about myself and God, I needed to untangle the lies about myself and God and break the unhealthy soul bonds that were created in those past sexual encounters or relationships. God also placed other resources in my life, in the form of books and an inner healing prayer minister, to help me break these bonds and gain greater freedom and greater understanding of intimacy and of my identity.

Through these resources I learned that, according to the Bible, God's design is for a man to leave his parents and be joined to his wife, and "the two will become one flesh" (Mark 10:8; Genesis 2:24). The man and woman are to bond into one.

---

According to brain research, when we experience intimate touch or have sex, our bodies release a "bonding hormone" called oxytocin. This chemical promotes closeness, intimacy, and trust with the person with whom you have sex, essentially "bonding" you to him.

When the sexual relationship is over and this bond is broken, emotional and spiritual residue may remain. These broken bonds can affect us as and create problems in future relationships and in our view of intimacy as we wade through insecurity, lies, and discontentment. Breaking bonds created by sexual experiences that led to abortion can enhance recovery.

Only God can break the bonds that were created in a sexual relationship and

---

* This material has been adapted from Paula Rinehart, *Sex and the Soul of a Woman: How God Restores the Beauty of Relationship from the Pain of Regret* (Grand Rapids, MI: Zondervan, 2010), 111–19; Barbara Wilson, *Kiss Me Again: Restoring Lost Intimacy in Marriage* (Colorado Springs, CO: Multnomah, 2009), 106–10; Joe S. McIlhaney Jr. and Freda McKissic Bush, *Hooked: New Science on How Casual Sex Is Affecting Our Children* (Chicago, IL: Northfield, 2008); and from the suggestions and prayer of my prayer ministry friend.

heal any damage so we can create new, healthy bonds in the future. To bring you to freedom from sexual soul bonds, here are suggestions I have gathered from various resources and my own experience:

1. Choose a date, time, and location that will be free from interruption and distraction. Bring paper, a writing instrument, a Bible, and perhaps a way to play music.

2. Prepare your heart to meet with God: I prepared through music and worship; some find fasting or reading from the Bible to be helpful.

3. Once prepared, invite God to show you what bonds need to be broken and help you write a list of the individuals from your sexual past, either by name or by description. Ask God to show you the emotional and spiritual impact of each encounter or relationship. Ask what lies you began to believe as a result (about yourself, others, or God) and what truth He wants you to have. I wrote about the grief and anger I felt as I released the lies I believed.

4. Pray a prayer of repentance and seek forgiveness (see a sample prayer below). If possible, pray this with a trusted, supportive friend or perhaps a prayer minister, as I did (see James 5:16).

**Sample prayer:**

Father God, in the name of Jesus, I come to You in complete trust. I confess and repent of my sin and the wrong choices I have made in this relationship. Forgive me, Lord, for entering into ungodly soul bonds. I ask for Your grace and forgiveness. In the name of Jesus, and by the power of His resurrection, I ask, Lord, that You sever the negative spiritual and emotional bonds that were created and cleanse and release me from memories and thoughts of ungodly sexual encounters and from their effects on my body, soul, and spirit. I renounce the lies that I believed as a result of my sexual experience. [Name the lie.] I receive Your forgiveness, Lord, and I forgive and release those on my list. Show me the truth about who I am in You, and make me whole again. Please restore the purity and innocence of my body, mind, and soul. Thank you, Lord, for forgiving, cleansing, and restoring me.

5. Praise the Lord for His forgiveness and restoration (see Psalm 116). Thank Him for your identity as a deeply loved treasure of God (1 John 4:9; 1 Peter 2:9).

6. To solidify the severance of the bonds, symbolically destroy your list. In my case, the prayer minister invited me to cut my list into pieces and dispose of them.

Note: If you have experienced any form of sexual assault or abuse, please consider seeking professional counseling in addition to completing this exercise. A list of resources can be found on page 179.

# FURTHER READING

The following books are recommended resources for you to consult as you continue your path of healing and as you grow in faith and your true identity in Christ.

## ABORTION RECOVERY

Abbate, Jane. *Where Do Broken Hearts Go?* Revised edition. Richmond, VA: Messy Miracles, 2018.

Freed, Luci, and Penny Yvonne Salazar. *A Season to Heal*. Nashville, TN: Cumberland House, 1993.

Layton, Pat. *Surrendering the Secret: Healing the Heartbreak of Abortion*. Nashville, TN: Lifeway Press, 2008.

## GRIEF AND SHAME

Brown, Brené. *The Gifts of Imperfection: Let Go of Who You Think You're Supposed to Be and Embrace Who You Are*. Center City, MN: Hazeldon, 2010.

McGee, Robert. *The Search for Significance: Seeing Your True Worth through God's Eyes*. Nashville, TN: Thomas Nelson, 2003.

Moore, Beth. *Breaking Free: Discover the Victory of Total Surrender*. Nashville, TN: B&H, 2000.

Moore, Beth. *So Long, Insecurity: You've Been a Bad Friend to Us*. Carol Stream, IL: Tyndale House, 2010.

Thompson, Curt. *The Soul of Shame: Retelling the Stories We Believe about Ourselves*. Downers Grove, IL: IVP Books, 2015.

Wright, Norman H. *Experiencing Grief*. Nashville, TN: B&H, 2004.

## SEXUALITY

Cochrane, Linda. *The Path to Sexual Healing: A Bible Study*. Grand Rapids, MI: Baker Books, 2000.

Ethridge, Shannon. *Every Woman's Battle: Discovering God's Plan for Sexual and Emotional Fulfillment*. Colorado Springs, CO: Waterbrook, 2009.

McIlhaney, Joe S. Jr., and Freda McKissic Bush, *Hooked: New Science on How Casual Sex Is Affecting Our Children*. Chicago, IL: Northfield, 2008.

Rinehart, Paula. *Sex and the Soul of a Woman: How God Restores the Beauty of Relationship from the Pain of Regret*. Grand Rapids, MI: Zondervan, 2010.

Wilson, Barbara. *The Invisible Bond: How to Break Free from Your Sexual Past*. Colorado Springs, CO: Multnomah Books, 2006.

## SEXUAL ABUSE

Allender, Dan. *The Wounded Heart: Hope for Adult Victims of Childhood Sexual Abuse*. Colorado Springs, CO: NavPress, 1995.

Langberg, Diane Mandt. *On the Threshold of Hope*. Carol Stream, IL: Tyndale, 1999.

Van der Kolk, Bessel. *The Body Keeps Score: Brain, Mind, and Body in the Healing of Trauma*. New York: Penguin, 2015.

## FAITH

Allender, Dan. *To Be Told*. Colorado Springs, CO: Waterbrook, 2005.

Benner, David. *The Gift of Being Yourself*. Downers Grove, IL: InterVarsity Press, 2005.

Cloud, Henry, and John Townsend. *Boundaries: When to Say Yes, How to Say No to Take Control of Your Life*. Grand Rapids, MI: Zondervan, 2002.

Jennings, Timothy R. *The God-Shaped Brain*. Downers Grove, IL: InterVarsity Press, 2013.

Kendall, R. T. *Total Forgiveness*. Revised edition. Orlando, FL: Charisma House, 2007.

Manning, Brennan. *The Ragamuffin Gospel: Good News for the Bedraggled, Beat-Up, and Burnt Out*. Colorado Springs, CO: Multnomah Books, 1990.

Meyers, Joyce. *Battlefield of the Mind*. New York: Warner Books, 1995.

Peterson, Eugene H. *Conversations: The Message with Its Translator*. Colorado Springs, CO: NavPress, 2007.

Voskamp, Ann. *One Thousand Gifts*. Grand Rapids, MI: Zondervan, 2010.

Yancey, Philip. *What's So Amazing about Grace?* Grand Rapids, MI: Zondervan, 1997.

## PRAYER

Eldredge, John. *Moving Mountains: Praying with Passion, Confidence, and Authority*. Nashville, TN: Thomas Nelson, 2016.

Hybels, Bill. *Too Busy Not to Pray*. Downers Grove, IL: InterVarsity Press, 1998.

Moore, Beth. *Praying God's Word*. Nashville, TN: Broadman & Holman, 2000.

Walsh, Sheila. *Get Off Your Knees and Pray*. Nashville, TN: Thomas Nelson, 2008.

Yancey, Philip. *Prayer: Does It Make Any Difference?* Grand Rapids, MI: Zondervan, 2006.

RESOURCES FOR MEN

Burke, Kevin. *Redeeming a Father's Heart*. Bloomington, IN: AuthorHouse, 2007.

Cochrane, Linda, and Kathy Jones. *Healing a Father's Heart: A Post-abortion Bible Study for Men*. Grand Rapids, MI: Baker Books, 1993.

Harper, Sheila. *SaveOne: The Men's Study*. Garden City, NY: Morgan James, 2008, www.saveone.org.

Rainey, Chris. *Healing the Father: Emotion and Spiritual Freedom from the Post-abortive Man*. Houston, TX: High Bridge Books, 2017.

# ONLINE RESOURCES

**ABORTION RECOVERY**

To further encourage you to share your journey of transformation with others in community, we offer the following list of resources to help you locate a local pregnancy resource center or abortion recovery program where you can connect with other women:

Abortion Recovery International, www.abortionrecovery.org
CareNet Pregnancy Centers, www.care-net.org
Heartbeat International, www.heartbeatinternational.org
International Helpline for Abortion Recovery, www.internationalhelpline.org
Overcomers Outreach, www.overcomersoutreach.org
Rachel's Vineyard Ministries, www.rachelsvineyard.org
Support after Abortion, www.supportafterabortion.com

**DEPRESSION**

Depression and Bipolar Support Alliance, www.dbsalliance.org
National Alliance on Mental Illness, www.nami.org/find-support
National Suicide Prevention Lifeline, suicidepreventionlifeline.org, 800-273-8255

**RECOVERY ORGANIZATIONS**

Al-Anon (for friends and family of problem drinkers), www.al-anon.org
Alcoholics Anonymous, www.aa.org
Celebrate Recovery, www.celebraterecovery.com
Overeaters Anonymous, www.oa.org
Rock Recovery (for freedom from eating disorders), www.rockrecoveryed.org
Sexaholics Anonymous, www.sa.org

**COUNSELING AND SUPPORT GROUPS**

Christian Care Network, American Association of Christian Counselors,
    https://connect.aacc.net/?search_type=distance
Christian Healing Ministries, www.christianhealingmin.org
Mental Health America (a list of various types of support groups),
    www.mentalhealthamerica.net/find-support-groups

# Notes

**Introduction: A Troubled Story**

1. Brenda Major et al., "Report of the APA Task Force on Mental Health and Abortion: Executive Summary," American Psychological Association, 2008, http://www.apa.org/pi/women/programs/abortion/index.aspx.
2. These questions have been adapted and blended from various recovery programs and my own personal experience. Variations of Post-abortion Syndrome signs can be found in many sources in print and online.
3. Anne C. Speckhard and Vincent M. Rue, "Postabortion Syndrome: An Emerging Public Health Concern," *Journal of Social Issues* 48, no. 3 (1992): 95–119. For more information, see Anne C. Speckhard, "Posttraumatic Responses to Pregnancy Loss and Abortion," accessed May 2, 2018, http://www.annespeckhard.com/pregnancy-loss---abortion.html.
4. P.K. Coleman, "Abortion and Mental Health: Quantitative Synthesis and Analysis of Research Published 1995–2009," *British Journal of Psychiatry* 2011: 199, 180–86; as reported in "Most Studies Show Abortion Linked to Increased Mental Health Problems," Elliot Institute, September 1, 2011.

**Chapter 3: Tame the Heat**

5. Gary Chapman, *Anger: Taming a Powerful Emotion* (Chicago: Northfield, 2015), 29. Used with the permission of the publisher.
6. Chapman, *Anger*, 58. Used with the permission of the publisher. In the next section of the chapter, I note two unhealthy ways of expressing anger. Both Gary Chapman and Charles Stanley provide descriptions of unhealthy anger. I use different metaphors to get at these similar concepts.

**Chapter 4: Climb Out of the Pit**

7. Cynthia Spell Humbert, *Deceived by Shame, Desired by God* (Colorado Springs, CO: NavPress, 2001), 21. Used with the permission of the publisher.
8. Curt Thompson, *The Soul of Shame: Retelling the Stories We Believe about Ourselves* (Downers Grove, IL: InterVarsity Press, 2005), 26. Used with the permission of the author.
9. Thompson, *Soul of Shame*, 48. Used with the permission of the author.

### Chapter 5: Surrender to Grace

10. Humbert, *Deceived by Shame*, 28. Used with the permission of the publisher.
11. Linda Cochrane, *Forgiven and Set Free* (Grand Rapids, MI: Baker Books, 1986), 92. Used within the publisher's standard of fair use.

### Chapter 6: Release Others—and Yourself

12. Cochrane, *Forgiven and Set Free*, 65. Used within the publisher's standard of fair use.
13. These ideas can be found in twelve-step recovery materials and in books by authors such as Phillip Yancey, Lewis B. Smedes, Vinita Hampton Wright, and R. T. Kendall, who all derived their ideas from the Bible. Their shared terminology emphasizes the importance of this aspect of healing.
14. Beth Moore, *Praying God's Word: Breaking Free from Spiritual Strongholds* (Nashville, TN: Broadman & Holman, 2000), 233.
15. Pat Layton, *Surrendering the Secret* (Nashville, TN: LifeWay Press, 2008), 90. Reprinted and used with the permission of the publisher.

### Chapter 7: Allow Time to Grieve

16. Jack Hayford, *I'll Hold You in Heaven* (Ventura, CA: Regal Books, 1986), 32–33. Used with the permission of the publisher. As Hayford notes here, "A biblical point of hope is present, for this [biblical exegesis on the lasting eternal being] means that your lost child is in God's presence, and you will someday meet him or her." See also Deuteronomy 1:39, Psalm 139, and Matthew 18:10, 19:14.
17. Hayford, *I'll Hold You in Heaven*, 62, 73. Used with the permission of the publisher.

### Chapter 8: Dare to Hope

18. Scott Johnson, sermon (2015) and personal correspondence. Used with the permission of the author.

# ABOUT THE AUTHOR

Wendy Giancola is the director of Past Abortion Transformation & Healing (PATH) at the Capitol Hill Pregnancy Center in Washington, DC, where she serves with and directs a team of volunteers within the PATH ministry. She is also a talented speaker and provides educational seminars in public, private, and non-profit settings.

Since 2009, Wendy has walked with many women, individually or in groups, on their paths to healing, and she has been blessed to continue as a mentor to some of these women. She continuously marvels at how God has transformed her wounded story of abortion into a story of His grace and restoration.

Wendy holds a master's degree in family studies from Kent State University and has additional training from Stephen Ministry and the Lay Counseling Institute. She lives in northern Virginia with her incredibly supportive husband.

## Author's Acknowledgments

With gratitude, the Capitol Hill Pregnancy Center and I wish to recognize the following individuals who influenced my education and growth on this topic and who, through their own books or programs, have provided hope, healing, and recovery to so many hurting women, including me:

Linda Cochrane, author, *Forgiven and Set Free*
Judy Cooter and Jeannie Stoner, co-directors, Abortion Recovery Assistance
Theresa Burke, founder, Rachel's Vineyard Retreats
Pat Layton, author, *Surrendering the Secret*
Luci Freed and Penny Yvonne Salazar, authors, *A Season to Heal*

I also thank those who established the twelve-step recovery process, programs, and literature, which provided a safe place for my healing and the groundwork for much of this book.

I also wish to thank the following people:

Doug, for the courage to bring the topic of abortion into the church, and Marianne, for embodying Jesus' compassion and forgiveness;

Janet, for listening to my story with empathy and showing me a path to healing—for believing in me and encouraging the creation of this book and holding my hand and praying for me the whole way;

Stacy, Lisa, and Melissa, the friends who supported, listened, cheered, brainstormed, and prayed with and for me;

Cheryl, the colleague and mentor who exchanged ideas, gave candid feedback on drafts of this book, and counseled me during difficult times;

The beautiful women who honored me with their healing journeys and trusted this project enough to share their stories in these pages;

The editors, designer, and typesetter, who contributed their considerable talents and incredible work to create this book;

Garrett, the book's packager, for taking a leap of faith and bringing this book to life and making it as beautiful as the women who are in it—for his tireless efforts, his long hours, and his patience and affirmations for me when I wavered;

Nick, my loving husband, for listening to my fears, my tears, my excitement, and every emotion in between, reassuring me throughout—thank you for not hiding from our story and for celebrating God's plans for it; and

Jesus, my healer and sustainer, for transforming my story into His story of redemption and grace!

# JOURNAL

# Journal

# Journal

# Journal

# Journal

# JOURNAL

# JOURNAL

# JOURNAL

# Journal

# Journal

Made in the USA
Middletown, DE
26 October 2023

41452870R00113